NORTON

CROWOOD MOTOCLASSICS

NORTON

The Complete Story

DEREK MAGRATH

The Crowood Press

First published in 1991 by
The Crowood Press Ltd
Ramsbury, Marlborough
Wiltshire SN8 2HR

British Library Cataloguing in Publication Data
Magrath, Derek
Norton
1. Motorcycles, History
I. Title
629.2275

ISBN 1 85223 545 4

Dedication
To Majorie Hayes (that was); who, to my knowledge, has never ridden a
Norton in her life.

Photographic acknowledgements
The photographs in this book were kindly supplied by: The National
Motor Museum, Beaulieu (pages 13, 16, 19, 21 (top), 21 (bottom), 23,
25, 27, 29, 30, 31, 33, 34, 43, 46, 48, 57, 64, 71, 89, 98, 99, 103 (top),
103 (bottom), 104); Andover Norton (pages 74, 119, 126, 128, 129, 130,
131, 133 (bottom), 134 (left), 134 (right), 136, 137, 139 (top), 139
(bottom), 143); The Sammy Miller Museum (pages 9, 12, 36 (bottom),
38, 73, 76, 91, 102); E.M.A.P. (pages 11, 45, 65, 66, 67, 72, 79, 81
(top), 81 (bottom), 85 (top), 94, 96, 105, 108, 113 (bottom)); V.M.C.C.
(pages 40 (top), 40 (bottom), 41, 49, 50 (top), 50 (bottom), 60); The
National Motorcycle Museum (pages 14, 15, 120); Castrol (UK) Ltd
(pages 53, 54, 55); Andy Savage (page 86); RAC (page 145); Charley's
Motorcycles (page 56); Bernard Hooper Engineering Ltd (page 133
(top)); David Davies (page 47); Derek Minter (page 111); John Robins
(page 110); Roger Bracey (page 90); S.R. Keig (page 62); Bob Graves
(page 140); Ken Sprayson (pages 85 (bottom), 101).

Typeset by Acorn Bookwork, Salisbury, Wiltshire
Printed and bound in Great Britain by BPCC Hazell Books, Aylesbury

Contents

NORTON: A BRIEF HISTORY

1898	Norton Manufacturing Company founded.
1902	First Norton motorcycle – 'The Energette' – produced.
1907	Rem Fowler wins inaugural TT.
1908	Model 1 ('The Big Four') introduced – first all-Norton motorcycle.
1909	First year of '3½'.
1913	Norton company bought by R.T. Shelley and C.A. Vandervell.
1920	Bracebridge Street premises established.
1922	Model 18 (first overhead valve engine) introduced.
1924	'The Year of Firsts'.
1925	Death of James Norton.
1927	Introduction and instant success of first overhead cam model – the CS1.
1929	Side-valve and overhead valve models improved.
1930	Model 30 replaces CS1 as basis for Norton race effort.
1931	Model 30 begins long run of TT successes.
1937	Double overhead cam version of Model 30 appears.
1938	Production concentrated on supplying WD16Hs for the war effort till 1945.
1947	Bill Mansell leaves company. Bert Hopwood employed as designer. Doug Hele joins. Roadholder forks fitted to all models.
1948	Dominator twin produced (export only).
1950	Featherbed frame used on racers. Double hat-trick at TT.
1951	Featherbed frame used on Dominator.
1953	AMC take over Norton.
1955	Big Four, 16H, 500T Model 18 and 19R dropped. Norton withdraw from World Championship.
1957	Gilbert Smith and Joe Craig retire.
1958	Lightweight twin – Jubilee – produced.
1960	650cc twin produced.
1961	750cc Atlas produced (export only).
1963	Company move to Woolwich. Slimline version of Featherbed produced.
1966	Receiver called in. Manganese Bronze Holdings buy AMC and Norton. Dennis Poore takes control.
1967	Commando introduced.
1968	Commando voted 'Bike of the Year' by *Motorcycle News* readers (1968–72).
1969	Company moves to Andover.
1972	Major improvements implemented for Commando engine.
1973	Merger with BSA Triumph. Norton Villiers Triumph.
1974	Collapse of NVT.
1975	Small-scale production of moped begins at Shenstone. Rotary engine development continues under David Garside.
1977	'Rambler' produced.
1981	First batch of rotary-engined motorcycles produced for military and police use.
1985	Norton goes into liquidation.
1986	Philippe Le Roux becomes Managing Director of Norton group.
1987	First rotary-engined Norton – Classic – sold to public.
1988	Commander produced. Company return to racing with assistance from John Player.
1990	F1 produced.

Preface

I think I should begin by saying that this book is not what it claims to be. It is not 'The Complete Story' of the Norton company and there are three major reasons why it is not: firstly, it is not possible to tell the complete story of such a company, its motorcycles and its ninety-year history in 45,000 words; secondly, it is not possible to collate all the information such an encyclopaedic work would require; and, thirdly, the Norton story is continuing.

I have tried to make it a comprehensive history and a fairly objective one: Norton did not exist in isolation and not all of their bikes were without fault (and that is still the case today). There is the usual caveat – that every attempt was made to be accurate but it is not always easy to find the truth behind events which happened ninety (or even nineteen) years ago. Much of history is subjective and many people who were personally involved in the Norton story were not always fully informed. In producing this book I have talked to people who could remember with startling accuracy events which happened fifty years ago and others who could not remember what happened fifteen months ago. It has been suggested that many of the former were just 'being helpful' and that their information should be taken with a pinch of salt. It's a point worth considering.

Too many authors would like you to believe that theirs is the definitive work; I would like to say that mine is not. I have noted inaccuracies in other marque histories and I don't see why mine should be different. In an ideal world that which is written down in black and white should be accurate, but anyone who believes everything he reads deserves the consequences. However, there seems to be more information being regularly unearthed and it will, hopefully, produce a clearer picture of Norton's history, but no one will ever know it all or be able to write it down.

As I write this introduction more changes are taking place at Norton: Philippe Le Roux has stepped down as Chief Executive of the Norton group and has been replaced by James Tildesley; the company is being investigated by the Department of Trade and Industry as regards 'company dealings' and an economic recession has affected bike production. Norton may sail through these problems or be brought down by them. At the moment information is scarce and political infighting and sensationalist reporting have done nothing to help. However, long-term plans and a move into light aircraft engine production (both masterminded by Le Roux) may enable the company to survive. Combined with the recent announcement that Norton plan to re-enter Grand Prix racing within the next year, it all provides a perfect demonstration that the Norton story is not yet finished.

Acknowledgements

I received help, advice and information from a great many people (and one small cat) during the researching and writing of this book. It's not possible to mention them all individually and, indeed, some asked not to be included here, but I would like to thank everyone who helped. Some people were more helpful than others and I would like particularly to thank Tony Denniss for his contribution; also Mike Jackson, Doug Hele, Richard Negus, David Garside and Philippe Le Roux (all, at various times, Norton employees).

I am indebted to Pete John for access to his library (from Ixion to Wodehouse); and to Andy Savage, Ken Sprayson, Derek Minter, Bob Graves and Sammy Miller for their assistance. Special thanks too to The Sammy Miller Museum, the National Motorcycle Museum, Castrol (UK) Ltd, RAC, Charley's Motorcycles and Bernard Hooper Engineering Ltd, and to John Robins, David Davies, Roger Bracey and S R Keig.

I must also express my gratitude to Pippa, who wields a mean red pen and has the highest regard for English as she is writ, for giving the manuscript a good going over. Finally, thanks to Old Puss Riddle for keeping me company.

1

Early Days

In the Beginning

The Norton story begins in 1898 in Birmingham, with the formation of the Norton Manufacturing Company. James Lansdown Norton, who had served an apprenticeship as an engineering toolmaker, set up the company to produce components for the booming bicycle trade which had been established in the Midlands. Although he was involved in the production of pedal cycles he was more interested in the possibilities presented by the internal combustion engine, then in its infancy. He had plans for a motor-assisted

Produced in 1905 with a 500cc Peugeot engine, this is probably the oldest Norton in existence. It is believed to have been James Norton's own machine.

1902 Norton. The ideal position for a motorcycle's engine had not been universally agreed even by 1902; James Norton had it more or less right with his Energette. Unfortunately, there are no surviving examples.

bicycle of his own design but these were shelved when he became involved with Charles Garrard, British importer of the French Clement engine. At the time, there were few successful British engine manufacturers and it was common practice to fit imported units to domestic frames. The hybrids built by the Norton Manufacturing Company could be supplied partly or fully built and were sold under a number of brand names; again, a common practice.

It was not long before James Norton produced a machine with his own name on the petrol tank. Called the Energette, it was little more than a strengthened bicycle with a 1½ horsepower (143cc) Clement engine 'clipped on' to the front down tube, but no better and no worse than most other machines available in 1902. This first machine was composed of various components bought in from manufac-

turers and suppliers in Birmingham and assembled by Norton. This system enabled the company to offer a range of models over the next few years, including a version of the Energette with a twin-cylinder Moto Reve engine, and other models powered by both single- and twin-cylinder Peugeot engines.

James Norton personally competed on the Energette in reliability trials and speed trials. He believed that a lightweight machine was the ideal 'for business, touring or racing' (as he stated in one of his early adverts). The Energette weighed about 70lb (32kg) and was capable of over 30mph (48kph). It was fitted with pedals, which were used for starting the engine and also to allow the rider to provide the euphemistic 'light pedal assistance' when long or steep inclines were encountered. The brakes were not particularly effective – the front one being little more than

James Norton at the Isle of Man in 1912. The bike is a Big Four and seated in the lovely wicker-work sidecar is James Norton's own father. Over the next few years father and son were to become almost indistinguishable with their patriarchal white beards and spectacles.

James Lansdown Norton

James Lansdown Norton was born in 1869, at the height of Queen Victoria's reign, in Birmingham. As a boy he was interested in all things mechanical and built a working scale-model steam engine which was the wonder of the neighbourhood. After an apprenticeship as a toolmaker he set up in business supplying components for the bicycle trade. He was then twenty-nine.

He produced his first motorcycle in 1902 and took part in various competitive events to prove its worth. He competed in three TTs at the Isle of Man even though he was not a particularly healthy man. He suffered from a recurring heart problem and looked much older than he was: at the 1911 TT one commentator noted 'Norton is a tough old sport and has the old age pension.' He was forty-three at the time. His white hair and patriarchal white beard, combined with his fatherly nature, earned him the title 'Pa' Norton.

He was a religious man and a keen member of the Salvation Army. In the early days of motorcycle production other enthusiasts would meet at his premises in an informal club. He was something of a visionary and made plans for a form of desmodromic valve gear (a system used by Ducati and Mercedes in the 1950s) and had even considered the possibility of nuclear-powered vehicles!

Ill health forced him away from his work for a year, leading to the collapse of the business in 1913. In 1921, on doctor's advice, he took a holiday in South Africa but spent it touring the country with a motorcycle outfit. The roads were often primitive and floods washed away more than thirty bridges on his route. The only failure he experienced was when a sidecar coupling broke after he hit a rock. The bike was, of course, a Norton.

Pa Norton died in April 1925, at the age of fifty-six. He left a wife and five children. He was genuinely respected by all who knew him. As a mark of this respect, *The Motor Cycle* promoted a shilling subscription fund which raised £1,203 for a memorial scholarship in motorcycle engineering at Birmingham University.

a standard bicycle stirrup brake – but efficient brakes would have been of little use on the roads of that time, which were generally 'smeared with a terrible green paste of pulverized horse-dung, rainwater and the assorted filth of an imperfectly scavenged city' (Canon Basil Davies, writing as 'Ixion').` Halcyon days!

The Peugeot engine's inlet valve was atmospherically controlled and positioned directly above the mechanically operated exhaust valve. The exhaust valve lifter was used for both starting and stopping the engine. The brass oil pump, mounted on the side of the combined oil and petrol tank, was simple but efficient – as long as it was not neglected by the rider.

Marketed in Britain as a Clement Garrard, the engine used in the Energette was a single-cylinder item with an 'automatic' or atmospherically controlled inlet valve and a mechanically operated side exhaust valve. It was bolted on to the front down-tube of the bicycle and hung off the right side of the frame with the outside flywheel more or less balancing it on the left. Drive was transmitted by a short chain to a small pulley which drove the rear wheel pulley via a leather belt. Hills steeper than 1 in 17 were a challenge, owing to the single gear. This had to be low enough to make starting the engine possible (there was no clutch) and high enough to permit comfortable cruising speeds without over-revving the engine. The drive belt was prone to stretching, slipping and breaking and to add to the enjoyment, the bicycle had no form of suspension. Later modifications to the Energette included the fitting of Druid front forks, to provide some form of suspension, and a slightly larger engine, a Moto Reve 275cc v-twin.

The First TT

Although James Norton was a believer in lightweights, it was a heavyweight model which gave the Norton marque its first major competition success. In 1907 the Auto Cycle Club (the forerunner of the Auto Cycle Union, the governing body for motorcycle sport) announced a Tourist Trophy Race to be held on the Isle of Man. The idea behind this event was to provide a proving ground for road-going motorcycles and to this effect a formula was devised which would prevent specialized competition machinery from entering. This included a minimum fuel consumption requirement (along with a minimum petrol tank capacity), the fitting of effective silencers, and

Rem Fowler and the V-twin Norton at the first Isle of Man TT in 1907. The makeshift pits were situated on the village green at the back of the St Johns' schoolhouse. The gentleman with the beard and the bow-tie is Rem Fowler's pit-attendant, James Norton himself.

the requirement that each machine should carry at least 51lb (23kg) of spare parts and tools. Twin-cylinder-engined bikes of the time were less efficient than singles and so the regulations stated that they had to be capable of at least 75mpg (4 litres per 100km), whereas the singles had to be able to obtain at least 90mpg (3 litres per 100km). The course was almost 16 miles (25km) long and included a variety of road surfaces, gradients, straights and curves. Each rider had to do ten laps, with a ten minute rest after the first five.

Norton's entry in this inaugural TT was a 'semi-works' affair with a Birmingham enthusiast, Harold Rembrandt Fowler, riding his own Peugeot-engined Norton but receiving assistance from James Norton himself. The engine was a 617cc, 45 degree v-twin, rated at 5 horsepower with lubrication provided by a hand-operated oil pump. The only 'tuning' it received was a pair of increased strength valve springs on the automatic inlet valves. This would have improved the high-speed performance but not the low-speed behaviour. However, Rem Fowler had been an active bicycle racer before he became involved with motorcycles, so he would have been up to the job of providing the light pedal assistance where required. Some assistance up the hills would have been necessary as the bike was fitted with a single-gear drive, probably about 4.5:1, though this allowed it to reach over 60mph (100kph) on the flat. The bike weighed about 180lb (82kg) and the rider plus load weighed as much again. Stopping it quickly from such a speed was almost impossible, since it was fitted with only a bicycle-type front brake and a simple foot-operated rear (a block of leather working on the belt rim). Often the only way of telling that these were being applied was from the noise they made, any other effect being negligible. Still, there was the braking effect from the engine to be had, quite considerable when correct use was made of the exhaust valve lifter. If all else failed, most riders knew the value of stout boots dragged over the road-surface!

Rem Fowler won the 'multi-cylinder' class at an average speed of 36.22mph (58kph), good enough to give him third overall – the outright winner, Charlie Collier, averaged 38.5mph (62kph) on his Matchless. Fowler's fastest lap (and the race record) was 42.91mph (68kph) and his average fuel consumption was 87mpg. Bare figures tell very little: Fowler experienced a number of punctures, one of which caused him to crash at speed; he had to stop on a dozen occasions to make roadside adjustments or to change the spark plugs; and at one stage he was forced to ride through a wall of flames caused by other competitors' fallen machinery.

Success with the 5 horsepower Peugeot-engined model was good advertising for the Norton marque. However, James Norton was already building engines to his own design and

A re-creation of Rem Fowler's machine, now in the National Motorcycle Museum. The original is believed to have been destroyed many years ago (having been run over by a lorry).

these he exhibited later that same year. Perhaps his own version of the Peugeot twin was not ready in time for the TT or perhaps he felt it was better to run with an engine that was a known quantity. In fact when the new model competed in the following year's TT it was not successful. Norton did win a number of minor events on the mainland, though; one such victory by Rem Fowler led to the Norton being labelled 'Unapproachable'. It was a description that was much used in later years and one which was forever associated with the Norton name.

The first all-Norton twin was similar to the Peugeot-engined model on which it was based but had a larger capacity (726cc) and a number of improved features. The magneto drive-chain became enclosed within a neat alloy casting, the single exhaust cam of the Peugeot design was replaced by a pair of cams and the general appearance of the engine was neatened. It first appeared with a single gear pulley but, following the general trend, it was offered the following year with an adjustable pulley system to provide variable gearing. Priced at 50 guineas, it was available from a number of sources including the London agents, Harrods and Gamages.

Birth of the Big Four

As well as the twin, James Norton had been busy on a single-cylinder design. This was introduced as the Model No. 1, indicating, perhaps, that he saw it as the first real Norton. It became James Norton's personal favourite and it stayed in production, in various forms, up until 1954. Although much modified over the years, the bore and stroke remained the same throughout (82×120mm) and the 633cc engine was always known as the Big Four (from its nominal 4 horsepower

The 1907 Norton used a 5hp Peugeot twin capable of propelling the bike at over 60mph (100kph), even with direct belt drive. As with the Peugeot single, atmospheric or 'automatic' inlet valves were used. For the TT, Rem Fowler fitted his engine with stronger inlet springs to improve the top end performance; in all other respects it was in standard trim. Fitted with a Bosch magneto and a Brown and Barlow carburettor it gave 87mpg (1,400km/100l) during the race.

rating – a system used to work out the taxation class of a vehicle and not indicative of its actual power output). A 475cc version was also made which was enlarged in 1911 to 490cc (3½ horsepower) and became the basis for the company's sporting range. It eventually developed into the 16H, which also remained in production until 1954.

'Taken outside Bob Meek's garage in Highgate 1917/18.' The bike is a well-used 3½ fitted with a number of practical accessories including a lighting set (with its acetylene generator strapped to the front downtube), a klaxon horn and a Cowie speedometer. The device on the end of the engine shaft is a Phillipson pulley which provided a variable transmission – a useful feature for anyone living in the Highgate area.

Old Miracle

Old Miracle was more than just a motorcycle in some ways, but in others it was less than a motorcycle. Old Miracle was the name given to a 3½ rolling chassis used by the factory to test the BS and BRS engines. In regular use for almost ten years, it was fitted with around a thousand engines and, at various times, held over 120 world records.

Engines intended for the BS and BRS models were sent to D R O'Donovan at Brooklands who would check them over before installing them in Old Miracle. The engine would be run in and the bike timed over a kilometre by a Brooklands official who would issue a certificate stating the speed it had achieved (70mph for the BRS and 75mph for the BS). The engine would be sent back to the factory to be fitted to a customer's chassis and the certificate would go with it. Any engine which showed special promise would be kept by O'Donovan for racing or record attempts.

As with the BS models, Old Miracle would originally have had only a single gear, belt drive and no brakes or mudguards. For track use only a Binks 'Rat Trap' carburettor was fitted. This was a crude but effective device which was really only designed to work with the engine running flat out. This was ideal for track use – it could not be shut off accidentally when going over bumps, for example – but impossible on the road. Old Miracle used a 1911 or 1912 frame (early frames had a straight top frame tube, post-1914 frames had a cranked tube to give a lower saddle height).

Record Breaking

James Norton's 3½ horsepower side-valve single was not an immediate success as a competition bike when it first appeared in 1909. But in 1911 its engine dimensions were altered (from 82×90mm to 79×100mm) and its fortunes also changed. That year Dan Bradbury became the first man to exceed 70mph (112kph) on a motorcycle of less than 500cc – his bike was the 490cc 3½ horsepower Norton. Other successes followed including the almost apocryphal story of Jack Emerson. Emerson rode his 3½ from Hull to Brooklands, won the 150-mile (240km) Brooklands TT (with no previous experience of racing), took a number of world records during the event and then rode the bike back home. To the chagrin of the Brooklands experts, he returned the following month and repeated the exercise.

The reputation of the 3½ was firmly established with the introduction of the BS and BRS model Nortons. These were bikes which had been tested at Brooklands by Dan O'Donovan and certified capable of exceeding a stated speed. Any exceptional engines were kept aside for racing or record-breaking attempts. The 'hack' frame which O'Donovan used for these attempts became known as the 'Old Miracle' and, at various times, held over 120 world records.

O'Donovan was kept very busy at Brooklands in the early 1920s preparing Nortons (often six or seven a week) and also Velocettes. He was joined by an assistant, Rex Judd, who took over testing and record-breaking duties. In 1921 a three-man team (O'Donovan, Judd and Victor Horsman) made an attempt at a twenty-four hour record (done in two twelve-hour stints); when his team-mates were overcome by fatigue, Judd carried on to ride most of the latter twelve-hour shift by himself. A new record – 60.7mph (97.12kph) was set. The 3½ was also the first 500cc machine to exceed 90mph (144kph) – with Judd riding – but it was deposed in 1922 by the overhead valve Model 18 Norton. In its first outing at Brooklands, Judd took the new bike up to 98mph (156kph) – 4mph (6.4kph) faster than the best 3½ could manage.

Rex Judd went to work for Douglas in 1922 and his place was taken by Bert Denley. Denley carried on the tradition of record breaking and became the first rider to cover 100 miles (160km) in an hour – on the Model 18 Norton. Record breaking at Brooklands and on the Continent was financed to a great extent by bonuses from the trade suppliers whose products would be endorsed by the record breakers. This practice stopped, and many riders and tuners who had made a living from record breaking went out of business in 1931 when the trade 'barons' withdrew their support due to the Depression.

Most enthusiasts familiar with the 16H will know it as a dull but reliable workhorse. Chosen by the War Department it was a popular dispatch rider's mount in the Second World War. Hard to imagine, then, that in its early '3½' form it was a highly regarded sports machine. One famous example, known as Old Miracle, held over a hundred world speed records during its long career.

James Norton competed in three consecutive TTs (1909–11) but had no success in any of the races. The company, however, con-

tinued to thrive and by 1912 had moved premises twice: from the original depot at Bradford Street to Floodgate Street, and then to Sampson Road North – all within the Birmingham city boundary. To give some idea of this expansion, it should be known that the Floodgate Street premises consisted of a converted three-storey house in which a total of eleven staff were employed; many of the manufacturing processes were still contracted out. Unfortunately, James Norton was not a healthy man and about this time a

Record-breaking with a side-valve single. Dan O'Donovan poses on an all-chain drive 3½ stripped for record-breaking. Capable of over 90mph (145kph) this track Norton had no front brake, no back brake worthy of the name and a saddle perilously close to the rear tyre. Riding it flat out at Brooklands must have been interesting.

recurring heart complaint forced him to take almost a year off. His competitors then were developing both their products and the art of advertising hyperbole (Norton's advertising was always modest, reflecting the man's own character). The natural result of this was a slide into liquidation.

New Owners

When they came up for sale at auction in 1913, little interest was shown in the assets of the Norton Manufacturing Company. Fortunately, they were bought by its chief creditor, Bob Shelley, who knew the true value of the company and the man behind it. His company, R.T. Shelley Ltd, had been responsible for the machining work for Norton and were, in turn, owned by C.A. Vandervell & Co. who had supplied magnetos for the bikes. A new company was set up, Norton Motors Ltd, and one of Shelley's directors was given the job of organizing the production of motorcycles. Bill Mansell was then in his early twenties and went on to become a major figure in the

Midlands' industrial scene. He was also an enthusiastic motorcyclist and already owned a Norton of his own – the right man for the job, it turned out.

The first move was to transfer all the equipment from Norton's old premises to a vacant building adjacent to Shelley's own works. This enabled Norton to use the parent company's facilities, giving them greater control over production and also increasing profitability. It was a fortunate move, for when Norton needed larger premises, after the Great War, another neighbouring building became available. This allowed them to move and stay close enough for Shelley's foundry to be their foundry. (The address of the premises they acquired in 1920, Bracebridge Street, became part of the Norton legend and, in the hands of the motorcycling press, a synonym for Norton.)

Sporting Sidevalves

Plans for a lightweight two-stroke – the Nortonette – were dropped and a 2½ horsepower (350cc) model was exhibited at Olympia that year, but it is unlikely that it went into production. Instead, Norton concentrated on the Big Four and the 3½. The latter was sold as a sporty TT model and was soon available in Brooklands Special (BS) and Brooklands Road Special (BRS) form. The BS model was a serious competition bike which was sold with

---

The 3½

The 3½ was introduced in 1908 as a smaller capacity version of the Big Four. Originally 475cc, it became 490cc when the bore and stroke were altered from 82×90mm to 79×100mm in 1910. These dimensions and the engine's basic design were features which were retained throughout its 46 years of production. The 3½ was not an advanced engine even in 1908 but it was well designed and well made. James Norton's personal motorcycling experience combined with his integrity and engineering skills to produce a good solid machine.

The cylinder was a one-piece cast iron unit held down to the alloy crankcases by four bolts. The valves were separated from the cylinder by an air space, which kept them cool and prolonged their life. For similar reasons, the magneto was placed at the front of the engine. The crankcases had internal strengthening ribs and the engine components were reassuringly massive. The flywheels were machined after they had been fitted to their shafts, a feature which contributed to a smooth-running engine. Lubrication was provided by a hand-pump fitted to the petrol tank. Modifications were made to the design in 1914 and some evolution occurred over the years, but the nature of the 3½ changed little, only its image.

The 3½ was supplied with single-speed belt drive initially, but it became available with a variable-speed Phillipson Pulley (£5 extra) or Sturmey Archer 3-speed gearbox. Brakes were minimal, even on the racing models – a frightening prospect considering the 90mph (145kph) capabilities of the fastest examples. In the first fifteen years of production – its 'glory days' – the 3½ was available as a touring machine (the TT model), a fast roadster (the Brooklands Road Special) and a real production racer (the Brooklands Special). The BS and BRS models came with a certificate proving their performance at Brooklands; in 1915 the BRS was capable of 70mph (112kph) and the BS was slightly faster at 75mph (120kph). At the end of the engine's competition life, in 1922, it held the world 500cc record at 94mph (150kph). This record was lost to the new Norton overhead valve engine which was, in fact, little more than a development of the 3½.

Old Miracle. This picture was taken in later years – when in use Old Miracle would not have been so smart and it is unlikely that a front brake or mudguards would have been fitted (never mind the bulb horn!). The carburettor is the infamous Binks 'Rat Trap'.

A very early 3½ engine. The Norton script (on the petrol tank) became more stylized around 1911 and the ignition advance control was moved to the handlebars; at the same time, the run of the top frame rail was altered. Oil supply to this engine is made via the rear of the crankcases but other examples have their supply at the front. A number of explanations have been given for this nonconformity but none is totally satisfactory.

a certificate to say that it had exceeded 75mph (120kph) over a kilometre at the Brooklands racing track. In fact, only the engine of the bike would ever have seen Brooklands, having been fitted to 'Old Miracle' in order to obtain the certificate. The BRS came with a certificate to show it was good for 70mph (112kph) but then it did have mudguards, carrier and toolbox. The preparation of the engines which went into these bikes was carried out at Brooklands by Bob Shelley's brother-in-law, D R (Dan) O'Donovan.

In 1914 some modifications were made to the engines which improved their appearance and, possibly, their reliability. These were partly a sales manoeuvre, but set the shape for Norton's side-valves for years to come. The following year the bikes were offered with a Sturmey Archer three-speed gearbox as an option. Despite the Norton's reputation

it was not chosen for military use in the Great War. The company were not really able to meet the huge demands that would have been placed on them, anyway. They had not fully recovered from the re-siting and restructuring that they had just undergone and were capable of producing only a handful of bikes a week. Bill Mansell did manage to get a contract, through the government, to supply Big Fours to the Imperial Russian Army but this dried up in 1917 because of the revolution. This had an unexpected but fortunate consequence for Norton: at the end of the war Bill Mansell learnt that there were hundreds of Big Fours in storage that had been paid for but had never got to Russia. Norton bought them back cheaply (many had been robbed for spares by the British army) and thus had a ready supply for the keen civilian market which sprang up after the war.

2

The Vintage Years

Home and Colonial

The end of the Great War saw Norton Motors Ltd in its Aston Brook premises, with a range of motorcycles based on two sizes of their single-cylinder side-valve engine. The Big Four was available with the new three-speed Sturmey Archer countershaft gearbox, kick-start and fully enclosed drive-chains at £87. The 3½ came in four different guises:

A Model 8 Brooklands Road Special (with Rat Trap carburettor and special paintwork) at the 1921 Paris Motorcycle Show. Guaranteed capable of exceeding 70mph (112kph) the BRS was little different from the 3½ used by Rex Judd that year to take the 500cc record at over 90mph (144kph). Not bad for £75.

A fully-equipped Big Four and De Luxe sidecar. With electric lighting, three-speed Sturmey Archer gearbox (and kickstart), speedometer, legshields and horn the complete outfit would cost around £130 in the early twenties.

Model 7   Brooklands Special (Stripped for racing, single gear, belt drive) . . . £80

Model 8   Brooklands Road Special (slightly slower, road-going version of BS) . . . £73

Model 9   Tourist Trophy (non- certificated Model 8, also available in chain- cum-belt) . . . £63

Model 16   Countershaft Tourist Trophy (fully enclosed chain drive, three-speed gearbox, kickstart) . . . £85

For 1919 the factory introduced a pair of sidecars, designed by James Norton (a keen sidecar man). The De-Luxe version cost £28 and the Sporting model was £25. The following year the 16H made its first appearance, so designated to differentiate it from the 17C. The letters indicated the Home or Colonial models, the latter having six inches' ground clearance (to deal with the rough-going so often found in the colonies) compared with the four inches' clearance of the 16H.

Despite the continued success of the 3½ (chiefly due to O'Donovan at Brooklands) the end of the side-valve's competitive days were in sight. In 1913 James Norton had declared that his side-valve singles would be good for 90mph (145kph) and they were approaching that speed at the beginning of the 1920s. The next step was an overhead valve design. There was nothing bold in this decision; many factories were already making overhead valve and indeed overhead cam engines, but Norton had no experience of overhead valve design.

Valves Up Top

James Norton chose the obvious route, which was to base the new engine on the old engine. The side-valve's bottom end was robust enough and producing a new top end would require less work than designing and developing a completely new engine. Consequently, the new engine had the same bore and stroke

Private entrants in the 1922 Senior TT. There was little success that year for official or unofficial Norton entries. The side-valve Norton was nearing the end of its competition life and the overhead valve still needed refining. Pictured above, from left to right are: Norman Black (retired 5th lap), R M Knowles (finished 15th), Graeme Black (finished 21st), W Hollowell (retired 3rd lap), Graham Walker, riding contrary to Norton's wishes – he was the official team's manager – (finished 5th), George Tucker (finished 22nd), mechanic Henry Horner (sic) and leaning on the bike A D O Carton (retired 4th lap).

The Model 18

When it was introduced in 1922, the Model 18 overhead valve engine already had thirteen years' development behind it. Or at least half of it had, for the Model 18 was based on the side-valve '3½' and inherited its well-proven bottom-end. The new top-end, almost elegant in its simplicity, was designed by James Norton himself.

The cast-iron barrel had a flanged base, held down by four short studs. It was well-finned, the fins becoming wider nearer the cylinder head. The cylinder head, also in iron, was a fairly simple casting with inlet and exhaust ports centrally placed. Early examples of the Model 18 engine experienced cracking of the cylinder head but this was cured by adding a dummy spark plug hole on the right-hand side. The rockers were carried on steel pillars to keep them clear of the cylinder head and permit efficient cooling. The rockers were supported on roller bearings and lubricated with grease. The head and barrel were slotted to accommodate the exposed parallel pushrods. Coiled valve springs were used, with deeply-dished collets. Short return springs were fitted at the base of the pushrods to stop them 'jumping' at high revs.

The Model 18 first appeared at Brooklands early in 1922, ridden by Rex Judd. It had been prepared by Dan O'Donovan but he did not have a lot of faith in the engine. His opinion changed when Judd took two world records with the bike – it was 5mph (8kph) faster than the best side-valve engine and good for 95mph (152kph). The engine was then kept under wraps until it appeared at the Isle of Man that year. In fact two Model 18s were taken to the island: one was ridden by Ralph Cawthorne and the other was ridden by Tony Vandervell (son of C A Vandervell, Norton Motors' chairman). After practising on his bike, Vandervell chose not to race; Cawthorne, who had had a string of successes on Nortons did ride in the Senior race but retired on the last lap. It seemed that the new engine could not stand up to the rigours of the TT course.

The Model 18 was improved after its poor début at the Isle of Man and went on to become very successful. In fact, it provided the basis for all Norton's single cylinder overhead valve engines. The last true Norton 500cc single, produced in 1963, had the same 79×100mm bore and stroke, and features which could be traced directly back to James Norton's first Model 18.

(79×100mm) as the 3½ but a different head and barrel. In the past, overhead valve engines had suffered from the problem of valve breakage: on a side-valve such a problem usually caused little damage and could be easily rectified; overhead valve engines, however, could be wrecked by the valve dropping into the cylinder. In the early 1920s this problem was solved by advances in steel technology which allowed designers to develop reliable overhead valve engines (though cost and conservatism kept side-valves in production for years to come).

The new engine used a well-finned cast iron cylinder with near-parallel pushrods recessed into the right side of the head and barrel unit. The rockers were held clear of the head to allow an efficient air flow. This was a good idea but, coupled with the engine's long stroke, did make it a very tall unit (a kink had to be put in the frame under the petrol tank to accommodate it). Coil springs which were used to close the valves and springs were also fitted to the bottom of the pushrods (to stop them jumping out). A feature of early engines was the relative size of the valves, the exhaust being smaller than the inlet – a combination which gave good acceleration but limited the top-end power. The exhaust pipe was swept out to the left side of the machine – the opposite of standard Norton practice.

In its first attempt at Brooklands, the new

Bert Denley with the Model 18, which was to provide the basis for all Norton's single-cylinder overhead valve engines, at Brooklands. The cushion on the petrol tank was a necessary addition, as Denley spent over two-and-a-half hours on the bike when he won the 200 Miles Solo Race in 1923. Four years later he was to become the first man to cover over 100 miles (160km) in an hour riding a 500cc machine.

engine set two world records. The 500cc kilometre record was raised to 89.92mph (144.71kph), over 3mph (5kph) faster than the previous record – held by a side-valve Norton. There was no success at the TT that year (for side-valves or overhead valves) but the competition experience did lead to some improvements being made to the new engine. Fitted in a modified 3½ frame it appeared at the 1922 Olympia show as the Model 18, price £98.

The Maudes Trophy

The strength of the new design was demonstrated the following year (1923) when Norton used it to win the Maudes Trophy the first year it was awarded. This was a trophy presented by Maudes Motor Mart of Exeter to the manufacturer who best displayed his machines' qualities in a particular year. The means of doing this was left to the manufacturer but the display was observed by the Auto Cycle Union. Norton's method was to build up a Model 18 engine from parts taken at random out of the stores. This was fitted into one of O'Donovan's track frames at Brooklands and after a brief running-in period the bike was charged round the track for twelve hours, breaking eighteen world records as it did so. Examination of the engine afterwards showed it to be in perfect condition.

Norton won the Maudes Trophy for the next three years in a row, and very nearly the fourth. The idea of the trophy (to test the qualities of standard road-going motorcycles) fitted in with James Norton's own attitudes towards motorcycle competition. The following year's test involved a non-stop run from Land's End to John o'Groat's – over 4,000 miles (6,400km) – with a Big Four and sidecar, again, the engine having been built up from parts chosen at random. During the 1924

The Model 18. There had been overhead valve Nortons (as prototypes or unofficial conversions) as early as 1913 but the first production model appeared in 1922. The frame from the side-valve model was used originally, with the tube under the petrol tank kinked to accommodate the taller overhead valve engine. It did not take long for riders to discover that the cycle parts were no match for the engine, particularly the brakes.

Phil Pike (seated) and Arthur Bourne (the ACU representative) with the Big Four outfit near Cullompton during the 1924 Maudes Trophy attempt. The outfit was later severely damaged in a collision with a charabanc; fortunately, neither man was injured and the bike and sidecar were rebuilt to enable them to go on with the attempt.

test the outfit was hit by a charabanc (a similar thing happened to the outfit involved in the unsuccessful 1927 attempt) but was rebuilt using standard parts taken from a local dealer's stock. Two overhead valve models were used in the 1925 event, over four well-known long-distance trials routes. Thirty-two long-distance world records were broken in the process. The 1926 event involved a well-used 588cc overhead valve model with side-car successfully climbing Bwlch-y-Groes pass in Snowdonia one hundred times in a row (the average gradient is 1 in 7 and includes a notorious 1 in 4 section). As if this were not enough, immediately afterwards it completed a 1,200 mile (1,930km) run around Britain. Although they were nearly successful in 1927, Norton did not try for the trophy again.

George Tucker with passenger Walter Moore after winning the Belgian Sidecar Grands Prix (600cc and 1;000cc) in 1923. Moore gained much useful information on the shortcomings of the Model 18 (although this is the 588cc version) by passengering Tucker in a number of events in 1923. A skilled draughtsman, Moore put the information to use the following year enabling Norton to achieve their 'Year of Firsts'.

Racing Improves . . .

The Norton team went to the Isle of Man TT in 1923 with some confidence. After all, the Model 18 was easily 10mph (16kph) faster than the old side-valve-engined bike. Unfortunately, speed is not everything, and the Isle of Man course showed that development of the cycle parts had not kept pace with that of the engine. One problem was the Druid front forks which the factory continued to fit to road

and race bike alike. It had always been James Norton's policy to compete with genuine production models, a policy not always followed by other manufacturers and one which, of course, would put Norton at an increasing disadvantage. The Competition Manager at this time was Graham Walker, a man noted for his outspoken and forthright nature. He was determined to demonstrate the deficiencies of the Druid forks although he had been threatened with the sack if the team bikes deviated

Tommy Simister awaits the start of the Senior TT in 1924, flanked by a pair of New Hudsons. The Model 18 was improved for that year's event, won by Alec Bennett – Simister came fourth. The Webb front forks were superior to the Druid forks which had previously been fitted but the engine was still '20mph faster than the cycle parts' (particularly the front brake). The value of the spark plug shield (on the plug lead) is also questionable.

from standard. He got round this by entering himself as a private competitor and riding a Norton fitted with a pair of superior Webb forks. The improvement in handling that this gave convinced the team that they too had to have Webbs and three out of the four riders changed their forks. It took the factory eighteen months to make the same decision – Webbs were fitted to production bikes in 1925.

Norton did not win the Senior TT in 1923 – Douglas did – but they took the team prize (second, fifth and seventh plus one crash-induced retirement). Graham Walker's fourth place was not included in the team results; he was, after all, a private entrant. It was the first time in eight years that a team prize had been awarded. Nortons also came second and third in the Sidecar TT, the first time such an event had taken place. Graham Walker, an official sidecar team member, piloted the second-placed Norton.

Happy Days

1924 was an even better year for Norton, one of the best they ever had, and the Model 18 was responsible. A number of other factors also had an influence, however. Bill Mansell had been placed in charge of the race team's efforts and he was determined that they should be successful. There was a sound business reason behind this: victory at the TT could lead to a three-fold increase in sales. To increase the chances of success he hired one of the top riders of the day, Alec Bennett, to ride in the Senior TT. Bob Shelley, the Norton Managing Director, employed Walter Moore as Chief Draughtsman and gave him the job of turning the Model 18 into a winner. (James Norton's health was forcing him to be less active in the company.)

Although he had only two months, Moore managed to turn the Model 18 into a TT winner. Few modifications were needed: chiefly, the brakes and the lubrication were improved. Norton had replaced the bicycle-type front brake with a drum brake, but it was far too small to be effective (one of the problems highlighted in the previous year's TT). Moore had a much larger unit fitted and replaced the hopeless old dummy rim rear brake with a Ford Model T 8-inch drum (there being nothing else suitable). This brought the Model 18's brakes up to the level of its engine's performance. He also experimented by fitting three separate oil pumps to one engine in order to improve the lubrication, but finally settled for one pump only, a proprietary Best and Lloyd item. It worked.

In the Senior TT Alec Bennett had an easy race. In his usual methodical fashion, he carefully paced himself for the first five laps, rarely using more than three-quarters throttle. On the last lap he caught and passed the leader, Freddy Dixon on a Douglas, and went on to win Norton's first TT since the inaugural 1907 event. Bennett's best lap time was 61.64mph (99.20kph) – the first time a TT had been won at over 60mph. In the Sidecar TT, it was a similar story: George Tucker was passengered by Walter Moore himself ('keeping an eye on things') and they came home almost half an hour in front of the next combination.

The Junior and Lightweight TTs were won by another Birmingham company, New Imperial, and in honour of these achievements the City Council held a civic reception. This included a march through Birmingham city centre and a banquet at the council-house with James Norton as one of the guests of honour. For his company there were more successes that year. These included the French, Belgian, Spanish and Ulster Grands Prix and the Brooklands 200 mile solo (500cc) and sidecar races.

The civic reception held for Norton (and New Imperial) following their successes in the 1924 TT. Pa Norton, although only fifty-five, looks about the same age as his own father standing behind him. Alec Bennett, winner of the Senior TT stands on the left of the picture, Walter Moore (draughtsman and sidecar passenger) stands behind Pa Norton and George Tucker (sidecar pilot) is on the right.

Nortons came first in thirteen top international events and, in all, Norton riders took over 120 firsts in hill climbs, speed trials and assorted races. The list of successful Norton riders for that year includes two men who later achieved much greater fame: Tazio Nuvolari, who went on to become one of the greatest racing car drivers of all time, and Joe Craig, who masterminded Norton's racing programme for many years. Justifiably proud, Norton commemorated their year's racing with a booklet entitled *The Year of Firsts*.

A Sad Departure

James Norton's health continued to deteriorate. In 1924 he took another long holiday in South Africa, following doctor's orders. However, he died in April the following year, at his home in Birmingham. He was fifty-six years old but owing to his illness looked much older. A religious, hard-working and honest man, he was respected by everyone who knew him, both in the trade and in his private life. As a mark of respect a fund was set up by *The*

Motor Cycle and the proceeds used to establish the Norton Scholarship in Motorcycle Engineering, Birmingham University.

Cams Up Top

A lot of changes took place in the two years following James Norton's death; not that he had held them back: it was just the natural culmination of a number of factors. The Model 18 continued to win races – Stanley Woods won the 1926 TT with one – but not as often

as might be wished. When pushed hard for the length of a race its reliability became doubtful and it was having to be pushed harder as more competitive machinery appeared. Velocette produced their first overhead cam engine in 1925 and this became increasingly successful. Other factories were already producing or working on overhead cam engines, suggesting that the days of the overhead valve engine were numbered, at least for racing use. The frame used on the Model 18 was a modified version of the pre-war frame and was now having to cope with a much more powerful

On display at the Tokyo Motor Show in 1927, the Model 18: a source of inspiration to the growing Japanese motor industry. By now the Model 18 had been improved, with a decent front brake and an external oil pump although this one still has the old diamond frame.

The CS1 (1928) was the first Norton of the 'post-Pa' era. It was modern in appearance and specification. It was, however, short-lived both in its competition and its production life.

engine and superior brakes. This problem was highlighted at the 1926 Ulster Grand Prix. Stanley Woods was leading the race when the front down-tube broke in two. Fortunately, the spark plug lead was pulled off by the movement of the frame, cutting out the engine instantly.

Norton's Chief Draughtsman, Walter Moore, knew the overhead valve engine had had its day as far as competition was concerned. He also recognized the superiority of the overhead cam engine. During 1926 he designed a replacement for the Model 18, retaining some of its better features but incorporating his own overhead cam design. Similarly, the need to replace the high old 'veteran' frame was recognized and a new cradle frame was introduced.

The old 'diamond' frame held the engine and gearbox suspended from the front down-tube and the point where the chain stays and seat-tube joined. The new frame was a full 'cradle' frame, with a pair of tubes running from the front down-tube, under the engine

and joining up with the seat-tube at the back of the gearbox. From here, a pair of tubes ran out to the rear wheel spindle to join up with the middle stays and the seat stays (on later models the middle stays were omitted). The old-fashioned flat petrol tank was replaced by a modern saddle tank, so called because of the way it fitted over the top frame tube. The new tank used a soldered-joint construction to overcome splitting caused by vibration, its appearance leading to its 'pie-crust' nickname. (Saddle tanks became standardized throughout the Norton range in 1929, the older open frame being modified to accept the new style tank.) Webb girder forks were used and 8-inch drum brakes (made by Royal Enfield) provided the stopping power.

CS1, ES2

Introduced on production models at the 1927 Olympia Show, the frame was first seen with the overhead valve 500cc engine and this

Alec Bennett is congratulated on winning the
1927 TT at a record speed of 68.41mph
(109.46kph). The bike is powered by the new
overhead camshaft engine – this one, a
prototype, is slightly different from production
versions. The gentleman with the trilby, on
Bennett's left, is Managing Director Bill
Mansell.

The CS1 was the top of Norton's range in the
late twenties. It was a short-lived model due to
its lack of racing success (the 1927 season
apart) and the departure of Walter Moore. It
cost around £80 in 1929.

combination was called the ES2, a departure from the usual numbering system Norton used for their models. (The reasoning behind this is uncertain: some argue that the letters stand for Enclosed Springs – the return springs at the bottom of the pushrods now being enclosed; others that they come from the accounts office, signifying an Extra cost Sports model.) The new frame was also used to house the new overhead cam engine (CS1 or CamShaft One) and indeed, with few modi-

fications, it was used on various models into the 1950s. It was a large, heavy frame but it did the job. Practice with the new ES2 at the Isle of Man TT in 1927 convinced the Norton riders that they had a winner. Until Walter Moore persuaded them to try the new overhead cam engine . . . Alec Bennett won the 1927 TT by over eight minutes with the CS1; its first race, its first success.

The introduction of the CS1 engine is an indication of the importance Norton put on

The CS1

The CS1 was Norton's first overhead cam engine. It replaced the overhead valve Model 18 at the top of the range and became the basis for their racing effort. It was designed by Walter Moore who had been brought in to the company in 1924 to take over from the ailing James Norton. Designed during 1926, the engine was first used at the Isle of Man TT in 1927. In fact, the engine had never been tested before. Walter Moore himself rushed with two newly completed engines to the Island, hiring a tugboat to get him there overnight, and persuaded the team to use them. He had faith in his design. And he was right, with Alec Bennett riding, the CS1 won the Senior TT by over eight minutes. Real 'Boys' Own' stuff!

The overhead valve Norton engine was at the height of its success when Moore began designing the CS1. He knew that the way to more power was through higher rpm and that an overhead cam engine was better in this respect than an overhead valve. Although high revs were important, the CS1 used the traditional long-stroke Norton dimensions (79×100mm). In fact, the crankcases, flywheel, con-rod, piston and barrel were all based on Model 18 components, modified to suit the new engine. Instead of a pair of timing wheels on the right side of the engine, there was a bevel gear arrangement driving a shaft which ran up to the cylinder head. Another set of bevel gears transmitted the drive to the single camshaft. The two cams were enclosed but the rockers were only partially enclosed, the far ends working the exposed valves. The rockers were two-piece items with screw adjustment on the valve end. Coil springs were used to close the valves. The oil pump was a design which Moore had first used on the 1925 TT bikes and was enclosed in the bottom bevel housing; a pipe ran from the front of the housing to feed the cams. The magneto, at the rear of the engine, was driven by a chain from the left-side engine shaft. As with the overhead valve models, the exhaust was swept to the left-hand side of the machine.

It is unfortunate that the CS1 did not go on to even greater things after its success in 1927. The engine proved to be unreliable, although it is said that this was due to Moore's attempts at improving it having the opposite effect. Increased competition from other manufacturers and more than the occasional spot of bad luck did not help either. Political problems within the company (Moore wanted a seat on the Board but did not get one) led to Walter Moore leaving Norton in 1929. He 'defected' to Germany, where he worked for NSU and, what was worse, he took his design with him! NSU brought out their own version of the CS1 and this, as much as anything, was probably responsible for Norton dropping the model. It was replaced by another overhead cam design, one which became much more famous and much more successful.

racing success. Racing was a form of advertising: winning, at the Isle of Man particularly, helped sell bikes. The late 1920s were a difficult time for Norton just as they were for other manufacturers. The Depression had brought about a slump in sales and a drop in prices. Manufacturers had to prove their machines' superiority on the track and also make them the cheapest on the market. Quality might be important, but price was a deciding factor for many people. At the beginning of the twenties, the Big Four cost £120; by the end of the decade this had dropped to just over £60, the Model 18 had dropped in price from £98 at its introduction in 1923, to £63 10s. in 1928 and then to £58 the following year. Even the new CS1, overhead cams and all, was a cheap buy at £89.

In 1928 Norton introduced 350cc versions of both the ES2 and the CS1, called the JE and CJ respectively. Neither model sold well and neither model had much luck in the TT that year. All five bikes entered in the Junior TT retired. What was more, fifth and sixth were the best positions Norton managed in the Senior TT.

The problems that sidelined the bikes that year were mostly of a minor nature and for the following year, 1929, the factory made few changes to the engines. Most noticeable was

Saddle tank, decent brakes and front fork, 'modern' frame, foot change gearbox and overhead camshaft engine made the CS1 an attractive proposition for the sporting rider in the late twenties.

the rerouting of the exhaust to the right side of the bike. One feature which became apparent in practice was the adoption of a positive stop mechanism on the gearbox. This allowed accurate sequential gear selection. Previous gearchanging required a well-judged kick of the gear lever: too hard a blow could push the lever through two gears at once. The system had been devised by one of Norton's rivals, Velocette, and introduced on their bikes in 1928.

Problems

Norton had no luck at the 1929 TT either: in the Junior TT two out of their three riders retired with broken valve springs, the third holed the piston. Velocettes came first and third with their overhead cam machines, an overhead cam AJS was second. In the Senior TT only Tim Hunt finished (fourth); Stanley Woods and Jimmy Simpson both crashed. Alec Bennett, who had ridden Nortons successfully in the past, wisely chose a Sunbeam that year and came second in the Senior.

After only two years as Norton's Chief Draughtsman, Walter Moore left the company in 1929. He went to work for the German company NSU. They had made him a very generous offer and he had become discontented with Norton (he had been expecting a seat on the board and didn't get it and his standing had declined with the fortunes of the CS1). Moore took the design for the CS1 with him. It was his own work, he had done it in his own time and he intended to produce a version for NSU. His departure, the threat of a possibly superior version of the CS1 appearing and the problems with the CS1 pushed Norton into coming up with a totally new engine. This job fell to Moore's replacement, Arthur Carroll.

Rejuvenation

While Carroll concentrated on the racing engine, his assistant, Edgar Franks, was given the job of updating the road bikes. Franks had worked for Sunbeam and HRD before moving to Norton. He had both practical and technical experience and a desire to do more than just 'tart up' Norton's elderly range. He started by improving the lubrication system on the side-valve and overhead valve singles. He did this by fitting a simple gear-type oil pump despite insistence by Carroll that his pump (designed for the new overhead cam model) was suitable. Carroll's system was fine for low volume production and a bike that would (or should) receive the careful assembly a racer requires, but Franks understood the problems of mass production better than Carroll. A similar problem arose a few years later when Carroll designed a primary chaincase for the Norton which consisted of two large steel pressings sealed by, in effect, a large rubber band. In theory it was perfect and in practice it could work well, but large-scale production allowed errors to creep in, and it was only a high standard of quality control which made it a production possibility. (In any event its efficiency was usually reduced by ham-fisted owners overtightening the large nut which held the two pressings together.)

Franks also re-sited the magneto on the bread-and-butter models: he moved it from the front of the engine, where it stuck out as though the crankcases were embarrassed by it, to the 'modern' position behind the cylinder barrel. This, more than anything, removed the veteran look. The cam follower and tappet arrangement of the overhead valve models was modified and the side-valve models received a pressed-steel cover to tidy them up. The rocker gear of the Model 18, designed originally by James Norton, was replaced by

Junior choice. Norton offered a pair of 350s in 1929. Both used the lightweight two-stay cradle frame but one was overhead cam (above) and the other was overhead valve (below). The ohc CJ (Camshaft Junior) was a smaller version of the CS1 and the JE (Junior Enclosed or Extra?) a smaller ES2 (although it used different valve gear). The JE was soon to receive Edgar Franks' update and the CJ would be fitted with the Carroll ohc unit. Both have a three-speed gearbox. The JE is in 'sporting' trim.

The 16H was 'modernized' by the addition of a saddle tank in 1929 but it still used the old diamond frame, Druid forks and Pa Norton's 'mag in front' engine. All this was to change with the 1931 model.

the system Moore had used on the 350 JE model. A flat, lozenge-shaped silencer with a 'fishtail' endpiece replaced the double-barrelled affair Norton had used for the past three years. Cheaper to produce, it also had a sporty 'Brooklands Can' appearance.

The old diamond frame was replaced by an open frame design borrowing the rear end arrangement from the CJ Norton. The new frame provided a shorter wheelbase and a more modern appearance: an end to the long, low, 'ferret' silhouette that had been a Norton characteristic. It was used on the side-valve and cheaper overhead valve models. The front down-tube had a slightly steeper angle to pick up with two lugs on the crankcases. The engine was used to bridge the gap between the front down-tube and the seat down-tube. The chain stays ran forwards from the rear wheel spindle, under the gearbox (much lower than in the previous arrangement), linking up with the seat-tube and engine plates between the engine and gearbox.

Variations upon an established theme pro-

duced two new models in 1930: the 20 and 22. These were little more than the Model 18 and ES2 with twin-port cylinder heads, a styling exercise which was fashionable at the time with other manufacturers but which did nothing for the bike's performance. Indeed, in later years, such models could be seen with one port blanked off (by an owner unable to find or afford a replacement exhaust) with no detrimental effect to the engine.

The new models and the modifications were first seen in 1930. They were exhibited at the Olympia Motorcycle Show as part of the 1931 range but were available in the last few months of 1930. There were ten different models in the range. These were made up from various combinations of three different engines in two different frames. This kept production costs down – particularly as there were a great many parts common to both the side-valve and overhead valve models – but still provided the customer with a wide choice. The Big Four was still available for the traditionalist sidecar enthusiast and the sport-

The Model 30

The Model 30 was Norton's second overhead cam engine, replacing the short-lived CS1. Designed in 1929 by Norton's Chief Draughtsman, Arthur Carroll, the Model 30 engine was used to power Norton's racing machinery for over thirty years. This was the engine that helped to create the legendary line of racing motorcycles which became known to enthusiasts worldwide as Manx Nortons.

Carroll's design followed the basic layout used for the CS1: shaft-driven overhead cam single with the traditional Norton bore and stroke of 79×100mm. However, in most other respects it differed, with a number of features being borrowed from a successful rival, the Velocette KTT. The Model 30 was not just an improved CS1, but a new design and, importantly for sales, it looked different.

The new crankcases had external ribbing to strengthen them and the drive-side casing now carried two main bearings instead of the one used on the CS1. The bottom bevel housing changed in appearance owing to the relocation of the oil pump. The pump itself was new and featured three pairs of gears – one pair for feed and two for scavenging – contained in a circular housing which was a press-fit in the crankcases. This was situated at the rear of the bottom bevel housing and the complete arrangement was based on the Velocette design. The bottom bevel and its bearing were located in a separate casting which bolted to the projection of the crankcases housing the bevel driven by the engine shaft. A two-piece vertical shaft was used to transmit drive to the cams, joined by Oldham couplings. This made the engine easier to work on and allowed for any misalignment and thermal expansion.

Drive was taken from the lower bevels by a short chain to the magneto, which bolted to a platform cast into the crankcases behind the cylinder barrel. The magneto chain was enclosed in a slim chain case which was to become a feature of all Norton's singles. The cam-drive, cambox and magneto-drive were also Velocette features. The latter made the Model 30 appear noticeably different from the CS1. Cylinder head and barrel were of cast iron (at least on the early engines), held down on to the crankcases by four long studs. The top bevel gear was retained in a housing similar to the lower gear and meshed with a gear on the camshaft. This bevel had a pin and vernier system which permitted easy adjustments to be made to the cam timing. This was a useful feature, allowing changes in carburation, exhaust system and fuel to be easily catered for. The new cambox incorporated straight, one-piece rockers which operated through slits on to the valve stems. The valves were closed by coil springs on the early engines but from 1934 'hairpin' springs were used. These allowed higher revs to be used in safety and, an important factor for a racing engine, a broken spring could be replaced without disturbing the cylinder head. The valves were lubricated by small pipes or 'quills' from the cambox which dropped oil in the approximate vicinity of the valve guides.

The Model 30 did not win the TT in its first year as the CS1 had done, but it won the following year, in both the Junior and the Senior TTs. And, more importantly, it kept on winning races for the next thirty years.

ing rider could choose the CS1. The depression continued to bite, though, and prices were reduced again in 1930: the Big Four was now only £54 and the CS1 had fallen to £79 10s. For those who could not afford a Norton even at such bargain prices, the company provided its own hire purchase arrangements.

Better Luck Next Time

Norton's new competition engine – the overhead cam Model 30 – made its début at the Isle of Man TT in 1930. There was no repetition of the instant success enjoyed by the CS1 in 1927, however: the 1930 TT was a walk-

Not Stanley Woods' year at the Isle of Man, nor Norton's for that matter, but 1930 was the first year of the overhead cam Model 30. Post-TT improvements turned the bike into a race-winner.

over for the Rudge team. Rudges took the first three places in the Junior TT and came first and second in the Senior. The best Norton position was third in the Senior TT. Any problems the Nortons suffered were only minor ones and the race team, managed by Joe Craig, sorted them out during the rest of the season. Some indication of the bike's potential was displayed at the Ulster Grand Prix and at the French Grand Prix, both won by Stanley Woods' Norton (although in the latter, it was the only bike to finish!). The Model 30 was to begin its run of success in earnest the following year and it would be a run unequalled by any other motorcycle, lasting for at least the next three decades.

43

3

Establishing the Legend

Bread and Butter

Norton entered the thirties with a modernized range. The revitalization had happened just in time. Motorcycle sales dropped during the early 1930s owing to the slump which followed the Wall Street crash of 1929. In these straitened circumstances manufacturers were not encouraged to improve their motorcycles, but to make them ever cheaper. Too many manufacturers got involved in producing cut-price models or tax-dodging lightweights. (A reduction in road fund licence for bikes under 150cc encouraged many manufacturers to produce 'Snowden models', named after the Chancellor who had introduced the concession. For some it was a road to ruin.) The competition between manufacturers to produce ever cheaper models was fierce. It was a path Norton chose not to follow: their updated range of bread-and-butter models, combined with their sound reputation stood them in good stead throughout the decade.

Their side-valve models had developed a good reputation in the 1920s and the continued production of the Big Four and 16H probably benefited the company during the 1930s as much as their most glamorous race-winning models. Sidecars became more common during the 1930s, being popular with the low-paid family man who needed transport but could not afford a car. The 16H and Big Four were ideally suited to sidecar use. One respected motorcycle commentator, Ixion, believed that the motorcycle market in this period had become distinctly polarized between the most basic model, often bought on hire purchase, and the top-flight machine, bought by those wealthy enough to be unaffected by the Depression. (Prices at the 1931 Motorcycle Show varied from just over £15 for a Wolf 'Cub' to over £180 for a Brough Superior outfit.)

Jam

The top end of the scale was represented, for Norton, by the overhead cam models. Norton enjoyed tremendous success during the 1930s with their 'cammy' racers and this was reflected on the overhead cam road bikes. This was fine for those who could afford them but it is argued by some that it had an adverse effect on the sales of the overhead valve models, the reasoning being that Norton were too busy concentrating on the overhead cam machinery to put much time into improving the rest of the range. These were considered 'second division' motorcycles. The public preferred bikes that they considered were not neglected by their own manufacturer. There is some truth in this argument, but it is an argument that was probably promoted originally by Norton's rivals, particularly those who did not go racing (or were not as successful), and thus had a larger budget to spend on advertising their own more stolid products.

Joe Craig; 'not a learned man', but he got results. Much of his reputation as an engineer was due to 'diplomatic' journalism and the terms and conditions agreed to by those who worked with and for him.

Joe Craig

The phrase 'he did not suffer fools gladly' is used to cover a multitude of sinners and has been applied, by more than one person, to describe Joe Craig. In many ways he was a hard man, uncompromising in his objectives, chief of which was to make sure Nortons won races.

His involvement with Nortons began in a small way, in Ballymena, Co. Antrim, in 1920. An apprentice mechanic, he bought a 3½ Norton and began hillclimbing with it. The 3½ led on to a Model 18 and success in his first road race, the Ulster Grand Prix, in 1923. His ability was noticed, and he became a works' Norton rider in 1925. In 1929 he was given the job of organizing the racing team.

He was not a learned man; his knowledge was gained through practical experience. He was lucky to have worked with Arthur Carroll and assisted him in producing the first Model 30 engine. His understanding of the overhead cam Norton engine stems from their complementary relationship: Carroll, the theoretician; Craig, the mechanic. After Carroll's death in 1935, he took over development of the racing engine and, apart from an interlude around the war years, he stayed with it until his retirement in 1955. During that period the power output of the works' Norton engine steadily increased from around 35 to 50bhp. Craig developed the racing engines in a painstaking methodical manner and jealously guarded his findings. It is not belittling to say that there were other engineers who could have equalled or even bettered his results: he was not a great engineer but there is more to running a successful racing department than engine tuning. He was a good manager and had a talent for spotting promising riders. It is a measure of his abilities that the works' Nortons were so successful for so long.

Joe Craig retired in 1955 and married Nelly Wijngarten, his second wife, the following year. He intended his retirement to be a temporary situation and planned to return to work, possibly in a consultative role. Unfortunately, in 1957 while retracing his honeymoon route with Nelly, his car went out of control caused by, or causing, the heart attack which killed him. He was fifty-nine.

And then, of course, there were plenty of machines boasting higher specifications than the Nortons, but few of them survived the 1930s.

1930 had been a development year for the overhead cam models 30 and 40 (500cc and 350cc respectively) and they came to the TT the following year with a number of modifications. A four-speed Sturmey Archer gearbox replaced the three-speed unit used the year before, the rear brake was moved to the left side and an Andre steering damper was used on the front forks. During the winter it had been decided that the bike weighed too much

and a lightening exercise was embarked on. Alloy components replaced steel wherever possible and the two-stay frame as used on the 350 replaced the heavier three-stay frame. The new overhead cam engine itself needed little modification. The cylinder head featured a down-draught inlet port (introduced after the 1930 TT and found to give better performance) and a smaller, 14mm spark plug. A lighter slipper-piston was also used. The revised racer had been developed by a team consisting of tuners Joe Craig and Bill Lacey, designer Arthur Carroll and rider Jimmy Simpson. Its development had been

A double second for Jimmy Guthrie at the Isle of Man in 1931. He is seen here on a 'semi-works' 500 entered by Nigel Spring (Spring is the man in the hat, standing behind Guthrie).

Tim Hunt's reward for achieving the first Junior/Senior double in TT history. The lady is his wife, who perhaps will be understanding about the oil stains on her white coat. Joe Craig, in silly hat, looks on and laughs (a rare occurrence).

sanctioned by Bill Mansell who promised them an open cheque book – as long as they didn't make any mistakes!

Better Luck

Norton's riders for the 1931 TT were Jimmy Simpson, Stanley Woods and Tim Hunt with fourth man, Jimmy Guthrie, a semi-works rider. (Guthrie's entry was supported by Nigel Spring, who himself had raced Nortons at Brooklands in the 1920s, been involved in record-breaking attempts and been part of the Maudes Trophy teams.) It had been decided that the work's team would ride to order in the Junior TT and that whoever was in front at the end of the first lap would remain in the lead for the rest of the race. This honour went to Jimmy Simpson. However no one had told Tim Hunt's father about this arrangement. His signals urged Hunt on and he took the lead, thinking that the official Norton signallers had made a mistake. Simpson had eased

47

Well-used 1932 Inter. The rocking gear pedal, the Brooklands can silencer and the wooden toolbox are period modifications. Hairpin valve springs were first used in 1934, on the works' racers.

off, anticipating little competition, but at the end of his fifth lap he was informed of the situation. He managed to get back in the lead on the sixth lap only to have his engine cut out. Philosophic – because this chain of events was not uncommon – Simpson sat by the side of the road musing about life when he was struck by an idea. Inspecting the carburettor, he found a very blocked main jet. He blew it clean, got back on the bike and worked his way up from twelfth to eighth place by the end of the race. In the meantime Stanley Woods,

who had been a close second to Hunt, fell back to fifth, owing to a broken steering damper. Fortunately, Tim Hunt was safe in first place and Jimmy Guthrie was close behind him, with a Rudge rider, Ernie Nott, third. This is how they finished; it was nearly a hat-trick, for Woods finished fourth. (It was later said, by those who knew him, that Tim Hunt was aware of the situation all along. He did not agree in riding to orders and believed only in riding flat-out. He was a dare-devil, not a tactical racer, and his riding showed it: 'neck or naught'. Joe Craig knew it too, and Hunt believed that Craig sometimes sabotaged his machines – in a minor way, such as leaving the plug lead loose – to give Craig's fellow Irishmen in the team an advantage.)

Four days later, in the Senior TT, Norton did get a hat-trick, with Hunt, Guthrie and Woods coming home in that order. In fact Nortons were first, second and third on every lap, and they broke the lap record eighteen times. Jimmy Simpson raised the lap record to 80.82mph (130.06kph) – the first time it had exceeded 80mph. Quite an achievement, for Simpson had also been the first man to lap at over 60mph and 70mph on the Island. However, although he put in such a good performance, he spoilt it by repeating his previous year's performance and was forced to retire after crashing. It was the first hat-trick in the Senior TT since 1911 (when Indian had won) and Tim Hunt became the first man

to win the Junior and Senior TT in the same week. A successful season of continental racing followed, with Norton winning eight Grands Prix, including the Ulster Grand Prix and six foreign TT races.

Racing Improves the Advertising

Not surprisingly, Norton made much use of their race winners in their advertising – advertising that had changed considerably since James Norton's day. In one edition of *The Motor Cycle* that year they had fifteen pages of adverts. Half of them were in conjunction with trade suppliers such as Renolds (chains), Terry's (valve springs) and even Tecalemit (grease-guns!) but Norton were not hiding their light under a bushel.

Road-going versions of the racers appeared

The ES2 in 1933. Hand change was still a standard feature but a positive-stop foot-change option was available. The gearbox was a four-speed Sturmey Archer unit, replaced on the following year's model by Norton's 'own' gearbox.

New for 1933: the twin-port 350cc Model 55. A smaller version of the 22, which was a twin-port version of the 18 (an ES2 in a loop frame – almost). Norton's mix and match policy allowed a wide range of models from a limited number of components. Appropriately enough, the 55 cost £55 in 1933. Not a hugely popular model, it owed its existence to a transient fashion and did not reappear after the war.

Pa Norton's Model 1 – 'The Big Four'. New for 1934 was the oil-bath primary chaincase, improved clutch, four-speed gearbox and 'race-replica' forks complete with check-springs. Alloy footboards were unique to the Big Four.

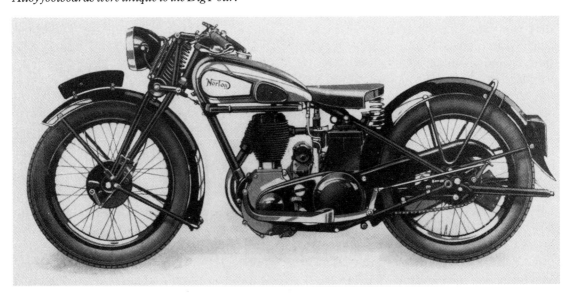

at the Olympia Show in 1931. The International, so called to celebrate the firm's international racing successes, could be had as a 350 (costing £82 10s.) or a 500 (£90). Very similar to the racers, these had their 7-inch brakes (both on the left side), the two-stay frame and four-speed foot change Sturmey Archer gearbox. There were a few differences: a cam and spring engine-shaft shock absorber was fitted to give the transmission an easier life (a new feature on all the road-going Nortons that year) and a pressed-steel primary chaincase was also used, replacing the very basic item used on the racers; the oil tank was of a different pattern and the road bike used a traditional rear stand whereas the racer had a light alloy centre stand. The 'Inter' was seen as a production racer and it soon became the case that improvements perfected on the works' racers would be incorporated in the following year's production model.

The CS1 and the CJ continued in production as sports tourers but they were noticeably different. Originally, they had been fitted with the Moore engine but now that Norton had stopped its production they were fitted with the Carroll engine. Sold complete with lights, they used the three-stay frame and a hand-change three-speed Sturmey Archer gearbox (four speeds, foot change or positive stop mechanism could be had as extras), and had their brakes on the right. Oddly, for 1932 the 350 used a right-hand exhaust port and the 500 a left-hand port (the following year both models used right-hand ports). The CJ cost £72 and the CS1 £79 10s.

All the 1932 models used hubs and brakes of Norton's own design and manufacture, the wheels being detachable and interchangeable. The rear sprocket was an integral part of the brake drum and the hub was fixed to it with three long bolts: a system which worked well as long as the bolts were kept tight, and one

which Norton continued to use (with some developments) for many years. To ease removal of the rear wheel, the back part of the mudguard was detachable. Wide, Webb-type front forks, made by Norton, were also a new feature that year.

Side-Valves, Twin-Ports and Transmissions

The major revision begun by Edgar Franks in 1930 had brought the road-going models more or less up to date. The side-valve models changed very little over the next decade although they received most of the improvements and modifications introduced to the range in general. The only specific 'improvement' of note was the enclosure of the valves first seen on the 1938 models. A chamber was incorporated into the barrel casting, fully enclosing the valves. There was an air gap, for cooling, on the inner side and a detachable alloy cover, allowing access, on the outer. Lubrication, previously part of the owner's maintenance ritual, was now provided by a hollow retaining stud which breathed oil from the timing case into the chamber. The price of the 16H rose through the 1930s from £49 15s. (lighting £5 10s. extra) in 1931 to reach £61 5s. (including lighting) in 1939. Interest in the 16H during that period may have been low but for the next five or six years Norton would be selling as many as they could make, as fast as they could make them, and the blokes riding them would not be paying for the pleasure.

Two new overhead valve models were introduced for 1933: the Model 50 and the Model 55. These were both 350s (71×88mm) and took the place of the JE which had been dropped from the range when the revision took place. The 50 used a single-port engine and the 55 a twin-port and both used the semiloop frame. They were effectively 350cc versions of the 18 and 22 and suffered from it. Although they were only 350s they had to lug around the same weight as the 500s. Consequently their performance was not sparkling: on a good day they would manage 70mph (112kph) – an ES2 was capable of 80mph (130kph) – and they lacked the uphill pulling power enjoyed by the bigger bikes. Still, they were cheaper: the 50 cost £53 and the 55, with its extra pipe, cost £55, whereas the 18 cost £59 and the twin-port 22 cost £62.

A number of modifications appeared on the 1934 models (seen at the 1933 Olympia Show and available afterwards). The pressed-steel chaincase designed by Arthur Carroll was fitted throughout the range. Allowing the chain to run in an oil-bath gave it an easier and longer life, but the presence of so much oil caused problems for the clutch. The old Sturmey Archer six-spring clutch was replaced by Norton's own three-spring item. A more oil-resistant type of lining material was supplied by Ferodo but Norton still had to fit a band around the circumference of the clutch to keep the oil out. The new unit incorporated an efficient shock-absorbing system and allowed Norton to do away with the spring and cam arrangement mounted on the engine driveshaft. The new clutch was cheaper to produce than the Sturmey Archer clutch but was still efficient. Norton went on using it into the 1960s (with some development) by which time it had to deal with much more power. It later became used on any number of high-powered 'specials' and it was even a favoured replacement for the idiosyncratic item fitted to The Mighty Vincent Twin).

Four-speed gearboxes were standardized throughout the range and a choice of hand change, foot change and positive-stop foot change were offered. An extra charge was made for the positive-stop option (the same

system as used on the works' racers). The engine internals were also subjected to some improvements. A second bearing was fitted to the drive-side crankcase to accommodate the extra power now being produced. After all, the overhead valve engine was a development of the side-valve engine which had been designed a long time ago. The camwheel drive arrangement was altered in an attempt to reduce engine noise but there was no noticeable reduction. The bore and stroke of the Model 19 was altered from 79×120mm (588cc) to 82×113mm which also increased its capacity to 596cc. This was done to reduce the piston speed, a problem when long-stroke engines are used at high revs. It also made the engine run more smoothly and improved its pick-up from low revs. Any identification with the special 596cc overhead cam engine that had recently appeared for sidecar competition use was purely coincidental.

Inter-Norton Races

The fine showing that the overhead cam machines had put up in the 1931 TT was not quite repeated the following year . . . but Norton had no real cause for complaint, either. In the Junior TT Jimmy Simpson and Jimmy Guthrie crashed and Tim Hunt went out in the second lap with a broken rocker arm. But, despite a strong showing by the Rudge team, Stanley Woods brought his Norton home in first place having been in front from the start. He raised the lap record by 3mph (5kph) to 78.62mph (126.52kph) and averaged 77.16mph (124.17kph) overall. The Senior TT brought an even better result for Norton: Woods, Guthrie and Simpson took the first three places. It was mostly an inter-Norton race (so to speak), with the Rudge team, once again their chief rivals, not getting

Smiles in the Norton camp. Woods (16), Hunt (30) and Guthrie (20) finished first, second and third respectively in the 1933 Junior TT. Standing behind Guthrie is Gilbert Smith; on his left are Dennis and Bill Mansell. Bill Mewis (mechanic) and Joe Craig are sandwiched between Woods and Hunt and the man on the extreme right is Arthur Carroll, Norton's chief draughtsman.

much of a look in. Tim Hunt went out of the race on the first lap this time, after he crashed into Braddan Bridge.

The 1933 season firmly established the cammy Norton as the top racing motorcycle of its day. Few modifications had been needed after the 1932 season: chiefly, a larger front brake, an improved steering damper and a bronze cylinder head. The works' 500cc racer

at this time weighed about 315lb (143kg), the engine produced around 32bhp and the bike was capable of over 110mph (175kph).

Nortons were unbeatable that year. Woods, Hunt and Guthrie finished first, second and third in the Junior TT, a race that was little more than a Norton benefit (Jimmy Simpson experienced the only setback when he suffered an engine blow-up on the last lap

Tim Hunt – whose real name was Percy, to which most names are preferable – with his 1933 Senior Norton (fitted with a left-hand twist grip, presumably for ignition advance control). Hunt's career was ended later that year following a bad crash at the Swedish Grand Prix.

while challenging for the lead). In the Senior TT, the order was Woods, Simpson, Hunt; all three averaged over 80mph (128kph), with the fastest lap going to Simpson at 82.74mph (132.38kph). Guthrie was placed fourth, only narrowly missing the 80mph mark, at 79.49mph (127.18kph).

The TT was followed by a tour of the European Grands Prix – the 'Continental Circus'. Two riders were entered in the Junior class and the other two in the Senior. Between them they scored firsts and seconds in the French, Belgian, Swiss and Spanish Grands Prix. The Dutch TT might have had a similar result had not Hunt, in second place, crashed on the last lap, whilst trying to pass Woods (the old system of riding to orders had been abandoned the year before). The Ulster Grand Prix also went to Norton but this time

included a local rider in the Senior race – Walter Rusk rode his Norton into second place, behind Woods, with Hunt fourth. Nortons took the Swedish Grand Prix a few weeks later but Tim Hunt collided with a Swedish rider in the 500cc race and suffered some serious injuries. A broken thigh that refused to heal kept him in hospital for nine months, on crutches for five years and out of motorcycle racing permanently.

New cylinder heads and barrels appeared on the works' racers for the 1934 season: the cylinder head used a bronze 'skull' with aluminium finning and the barrel had aluminium finning with a steel liner. The size of the finning on both was increased to deal with the extra heat produced. Hairpin valve springs were also used for the first time that year. Valve springs were still a problem for racing engines, being prone to breaking due to continual high revs and 'going off' during long races. Hairpin springs permitted the use of higher revs, were reckoned to be more reliable and could be replaced very quickly – without the cylinder head having to be removed, as was the case with coil springs. Megaphone exhaust systems were tried out (instead of the straight pipe normally used) and so was a twin-plug head (the second spark-plug was virtually obscured by the cam drive-gear and could only be replaced by removing the cambox itself). A new method of retaining the petrol tank was also introduced: four rubber-bushed bolts running through vertical tubes in the tank were secured to horizontal frame lugs underneath it, effectively isolating it from engine vibration. Vibration was becoming a problem on the racers: the following year the works' bikes were fitted with a pair of head-steadies running from the front of the cylinder head to the front down-tube and the front engine mountings were strengthened.

Down and Out

No great changes had been made to the bikes for the 1934 season, but then none were needed: Guthrie and Simpson took first and second in both the Junior and the Senior TT. Stanley Woods set fastest lap in the Senior but not for Norton: he had 'gone over' to the Swedish company Husqvarna, riding one of their v-twins. His place in the team and that of the injured Tim Hunt were taken by Walter Handley and Charlie Dodson, both experienced riders. They were valuable additions to the Norton team, particularly after Guthrie fell and broke his arm in the Dutch TT, and came first and second respectively in the Belgian Grand Prix. Other successes for Norton that year included wins in the Belgian, Swiss and German Grands Prix and the Dutch TT. Despite another good year with Norton, Jimmy Simpson retired from racing at the end of 1934. He had ridden at the Isle of Man twelve times for Norton but his only TT win had been in his final year, in the Junior event on a 250cc Rudge. He is remembered, however, for being the first man to lap the Island at 60, 70 and 80mph (97, 113 and 129kph); a feat which spanned incredible differences in racing machinery and conditions, the likes of which would never be seen again.

The International models continued to benefit from the racers' development. The 1933 Inters appeared with the rebound-spring system which Carroll had used to improve the racers' front forks. It was not a new idea but Carroll's adaptation of it worked well enough for Ariel and Triumph to introduce their own version a few years later. The bimetallic head was offered as an option in the same year but was only of real value if the bike were to be raced; for road use the cast-iron head was more practical. Inside the cambox, the rockers were increased in size, as were their

bearings, and an oil feed to the valve guides was introduced. On the cycle-parts side, the wheel rims, spokes and brake drums were chrome-plated, which, if nothing else, made them sparkle. The following year the front hubs were replaced by the narrower type currently used on the works' bikes, along with their narrower forks. Available to a lucky (wealthy) few, the Inter Norton was one of the top road-bikes of its day. A big, handsome machine, it cost £90 (£30 more than the

Joe Craig helps Jimmy Guthrie get under way at the Ulster Grand Prix in 1934. Guthrie won the Junior and Senior TTs that year but the Ulster GP went to his team mate, Jimmy Simpson. Fitting really, as Simpson was runner up to Guthrie in both Isle of Man events.

The Inter

'No motorcycle has ever before offered such incontestable proof of all-round excellence as the 1932 Norton.' Advertising hyperbole, perhaps, but Norton had plenty to be proud of when they introduced the International at the Olympia Motorcycle Show in 1931. They had won fifteen international road races that year and the new model was a 'genuine TT replica' and 'incorporated all the latest Norton practice' according to *The Motorcycle*.

The Inter *was* Norton's TT replica and one of the fastest bikes on the road – good for 90mph (140kph) in standard trim. It could be ordered in road-going (electric lighting £5 10s. extra) or racing specification. Alloy head and barrel, straight-through exhaust pipe, open front chain guard, racing gearbox (no kickstart), three-plate clutch and 14mm spark plug were just some of the options that were available. The serious racing man could send his Inter back to the factory each year to have it overhauled and updated to the latest specification.

Not surprisingly, the Inter wasn't cheap: the Model 30 (490cc) cost £90 in 1932 and the Model 40 (348cc) cost £82 10s. By comparison, the top-of-the-range models from Rudge and Vincent-H.R.D. cost £70 and £74 respectively.

A Model 40 Inter in racing trim, supplied to Layton's of Oxford in August 1936, possibly for that year's Manx Grand Prix. Optional equipment fitted included alloy head and barrel, dull plated petrol tank, racing gearbox and central oil-feed to rocker box. The bike was returned to the factory over the next two years for updating, at which point the later cylinder head and barrel and plunger suspension were fitted.

plebeian Model 18 and over £40 more than the humble 16H).

The 1935 works' bikes were the first to use Norton's own gearbox. The Sturmey Archer gearbox traditionally used had been made by Raleigh but in 1934 they stopped production to concentrate on their three-wheeled commercial vehicle. Norton arranged to have it made by another gearbox manufacturer, Burman, incorporating a few improvements of their own. These, basically, enabled it to handle the extra power produced by the racers and improved the gear selection process. With only relatively minor modifications, Norton used the same design for the next forty years. Other new features on the works' bikes that year included alloy cooling fins on the brake drums and enclosed valve-gear mechanism.

Jimmy Guthrie had new team mates at the 1935 TT. Walter Rusk and Johnny Duncan replaced Tim Hunt and Jimmy Simpson in the official Norton team and John, better known as 'Crasher', White was an additional rider in the Junior TT. White had earned the nickname Crasher as a member of 'The Quacks' (Cambridge University Auto Club). Crashing in the 1933 Junior Manx Grand Prix – whilst leading – and twice in the Senior only consolidated his right to the title. Despite his reputation and his record, he did win the Junior Manx the next year, with a bike that was suspiciously similar to the works' models. (The Manx was an amateur event and works' machinery was not permitted.)

Tactics

The Junior event was, once again, a Norton benefit. There was a strong challenge from the Velocette team with their cammy singles (relatives, albeit illegitimately, of the Norton)

Jimmy Simpson passes Harry Newman (Velocette) at Clady Corner on his way to winning the 1934 Ulster Grand Prix. He set eight lap records at the Isle of Man and was the first man to lap at 60, 70 and 80mph (97, 113 and 129kph); he also established a record as a 'bike breaker' – setting fast times, but failing to finish.

but the Norton riders pulled off another hat-trick. High winds prevented any new records being set, but Guthrie, Rusk and White, in that order, led from start to finish; Johnny Duncan's seventh place helped Norton to take the team prize.

The main challenge in the Senior TT came from ex-Norton rider Stanley Woods. Woods rode a Moto Guzzi v-twin that year, a bike known to be as fast as the Nortons but, perhaps, less suited to the conditions found in TT racing. It was a close race but Guthrie showed his determination from the start by breaking the lap record on the first lap, then on the second and then on the third. Woods tagged behind, in second place. On the sixth, the penultimate lap, Guthrie had a twenty-six second lead over Woods – enough of a margin, it was felt in the Norton camp, for their man to be able to take it a little easier (and so preserve the engine), especially as Woods' pit

The 1935 works Norton as ridden by Jimmy Guthrie, 310lb (141kg), 32bhp at 5,500rpm and 110mph (176kph) are the vital statistics of the single cam works 500. Not the most technologically advanced machine perhaps, but good enough to take Norton's riders to victories at the Swiss, Dutch, German, Spanish, Belgian and Ulster Grands Prix that year.

crew were preparing for their rider to come in for extra fuel (Guthrie had taken his on board in the fourth lap). Guthrie received the signal and eased up, but instead of stopping for fuel, Woods went straight past his pit, flat out after the Norton. Guthrie finished first and the immediate assumption was that he had won, but as it had been a staggered start no one could be sure until Woods finished. It was nearly fifteen minutes before Woods finished his race and only the official timekeepers really knew who the winner was: Woods, by four seconds. Four seconds in a race lasting more than three hours! Woods' last lap was completed at a speed of 86.53mph (138.45kph), better than any of Guthrie's and better, even than the previous record, set by Woods himself on a Norton in 1933. Woods' success was due to his riding skill, his Moto

Guzzi and his forward thinking but it was also due to his superior timing and signalling system, which gave him a better understanding of the race, and to good luck: at the end of the race his petrol tank was empty, the only fuel was in the carburettors! If the race had been any longer, . . . if Guthrie had not eased-up on the last lap . . .

Continental victories followed and although Nortons won both their classes at the Swiss Grand Prix they received a sign that they might not always have it all their own way. The 350cc race was held concurrently with the 250cc race and a works' DKW two-stroke in that event beat both Nortons to the finish. A real defeat came at the Ulster Grand Prix where Velocettes came first and second in the Junior event, although Guthrie did win the Senior race.

Rear Springing

For the 1936 racing season Norton introduced a number of changes in an attempt to keep their bikes in front of the opposition. Most obvious of these was the modified frame with its 'plunger' rear suspension. In this, the rear stays were altered to finish well above and below the wheel spindle but were connected by a bridge piece. At the end of each stay was a tubular bracket, machined to accept a steel piston or 'plunger', its up and down movement being controlled by springs in the brackets. It was similar to systems which had been used in car suspension for many years but was inferior to certain systems already used by other motorcycle manufacturers, such as HRD and Moto Guzzi. It had an adverse effect upon the drive chain and provided little up and down movement, but it was better than nothing. Not obvious was the increase in engine capacities achieved by increasing the bore of the Model 30 to 79.6mm (499cc) and changing the bore and stroke of the Model 40 to 73.4×82.5mm (349cc). Nothing earth-shattering there but at least it looked as though Norton were doing something and pyschological advantages can be valuable. Anyway, the real changes were to come the following year.

Walter Rusk was unable to ride that year because of a broken arm, and his place in the team was taken by Freddie Frith. A wise choice: Frith won the Junior TT (his first TT), overcoming a strong challenge from Velocette with their new double overhead cam engine. Crasher White came second and Guthrie was also second – or not: Guthrie had been forced to stop whilst leading, owing to his rear chain jumping a sprocket (probably a side-effect of the plunger suspension). The stewards were informed that he had received assistance to restart the bike, and this was not permitted in the race regulations. He was thus disqualified but continued the race and finished behind the winner and in front of White. On consideration of his protest the stewards granted an award of equivalent value to the second prize but did not include Guthrie in the list of finishers. He made up for it in the Senior race: a real contest with Stanley Woods (now riding a Velocette). Both riders broke the lap record and were never far apart. Guthrie took the lead from the start but it was a slender lead and Woods' sixth lap was the fastest of the race – did Woods have another trick to play? No, but fate did: the Velocette's engine developed a misfire and Guthrie won by eighteen seconds. Woods was second with Frith and White coming in behind him.

As the 1930s drew to a close, Norton faced increasing competition on the race tracks. Their single-cylinder engines were at a disadvantage against the new crop of racing motorcycles. Continental manufacturers were developing powerful multis using superchargers to boost power output to levels that Norton could not reach with their single. Even at the start of the 1930s it was acknowledged that multis were superior but Norton's philosophy was to race bikes like those they sold to the public: a fine ideal and typical of James Norton's attitude, but times were changing and the Norton approach was becoming somewhat quixotic. However, Norton had plenty of experience with singles and, on the right course, in the right hands, they would remain a match for the blown multis – for a while.

In the meantime, the International models continued to benefit from the racers' evolution. It might be argued that this was evidence that 'racing improves the breed' but it is just as true that Norton's bread-and-butter range received few race-tested improvements.

59

Still, the International was closely identified with the racers and was available to anyone (anyone who could afford it, that is). In 1935 the identification was carried even further. That year Norton offered the Inter in racing trim: hairpin valve springs, special cylinder head, engine prepared by the racing department, their own gearbox (as used in the TT), racing petrol tank (including the rubber chin-pad for when the rider really 'got down to it') and the various specialized bits and pieces which turn a production road bike into a real racer. Handlebars became rubber-mounted (trying to hide the vibration problem) and the flat, fantail silencer was replaced by a tubular item (or, as an option, the racer's straight-through pipe).

Few changes were introduced the following year (alloy barrel, 14mm spark plugs) but the new plunger frame became available at the end of 1938 for an extra £15. In full race spec,

and now with Elektron crankcases, the Model 30 cost £123 9s. 6d., ready to race. The racing version was still called an International but in 1939, to distinguish it from the road-going Inter, Norton's production racer was listed as the Manx Grand Prix Model; it became known to enthusiasts everywhere simply as 'The Manx'.

Two Camshafts are Better than One?

The quest for more power led Norton to produce a double overhead cam cylinder head for the 1937 season (just as Velocette had done the year before). The new design looked impressive, with its increased finning and redesigned cambox. Inside the cambox, drive from the vertical shaft was transmitted by a train of gears to the two camshafts. Vernier

At the opposite end of the scale from the Big Four came the Inter. A real race replica, it wasn't cheap but it was one of the fastest bikes on the road – the Model 30 in 1934 cost £90 and reached 90mph (145kph.)

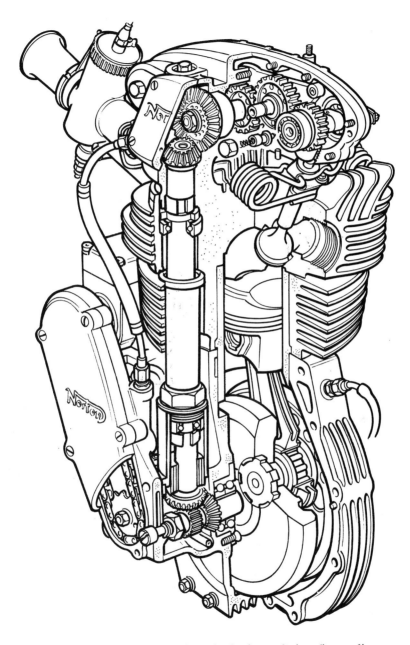

The overhead cam 'Manx' Norton engine was 'dated from the day it was designed' according to some critics. Still, Norton fought a very successful rearguard action with it for nearly thirty years. Of course, many other factors played a part in its prolonged success but the Manx was one of the few Grand Prix machines available to the ordinary racing man. For many years after it ceased production it continued to be a prerequisite for success in the 500cc class. Seen here in cutaway form is the 1957 Model 30 engine.

A modest smile from the elegant Freddie Frith, second-placed man in the 1937 Junior TT.
He had more to smile about later in the week when he won the Senior event. This was the first
year of the 'double knocker' Norton.

coupling systems were used on the central gear and the actual camshaft gears to permit valve timing adjustments. Each cam operated a short tappet through a bush in the cambox to open the valves, exposed hairpin springs closing them. Unfortunately, the new design did not perform according to plan at the TT and a slightly modified single-cam system was secretly rigged up inside the new cambox. The factory also experimented with another design which used coil springs and had fully enclosed valves. Oil-tight, but not as powerful as the normal set-up (the coil springs restricted the rpm), it powered Jack Williams to tenth place in both races and was then shelved.

The Junior TT saw another walkover by the Norton team: Guthrie, Frith and White were first, second and third. Stanley Woods picked up fourth place for Velocette and Harold Daniell came fifth.

Things were not quite so easy in the Senior. Stanley Woods was entered on Velocette's new 500cc twin-cam MTT; Italian champion Omobono Tenni had one of Moto Guzzi's very quick v-twins and Jock West was riding a supercharged BMW twin – a bike with tremendous power but not, perhaps, the handling to match. Nortons started the race well with Guthrie going into the lead on the first lap, with Frith in second place. Woods passed Frith on the second lap and looked set to challenge Guthrie. Strung out in order behind them were West, White and Tenni – an interesting situation. The battle for first place was decided on the fifth lap when Guthrie's engine blew up, giving Woods the lead. Tenni went out on the same lap and West dropped back with a fuel leak. Aware of Guthrie's misfortune, Frith put in a tremendous effort to catch up with Woods on the sixth lap, both of them lapping at a record 87.88mph (140.61kph). Ten minutes in front of Frith, because of the staggered start, Woods received warning of Frith's performance from his signallers. Managing to pull out the extra effort needed, he upped his last-lap speed to 88.09mph (140.94kph). Then Woods had to wait for Frith to finish (as Guthrie had waited for him in 1935) before he would know who had won. Frith knew what was required and he did it: 90.27mph (144.43kph). He had won by just fifteen seconds: a brilliant ride, a new record and another win for Norton.

'A True Sportsman'

The usual round of continental meetings followed, with the Nortons once more displaying their superiority. Particularly pleasing for Guthrie was the Swiss Grand Prix, where he won both Junior and Senior events. This also made him a double European Champion: the European Grand Prix was a 'movable feast', with the Swiss meeting being its home that year. Less successful was the German Grand Prix at the close of the season. The Norton riders faced a strong challenge from the blown BMWs, NSUs, and two-stroke DKWs, all eager to win in front of a home crowd. In the senior race, Frith's engine would not run properly and Guthrie got away to a bad start. He made up for it, though, and worked his way to the front of the field, holding the lead

until the last lap. With victory in sight and only a mile to go, Guthrie crashed. It was later rumoured that he had been forced to avoid another rider; another source claimed that hot tar and loose sand had caused the accident (on a tricky bend) and years later one of the team's mechanics stated that the rear wheel spindle had broken. Whatever the reason, Jimmy Guthrie received serious head injuries in the accident and died in hospital a few hours later. Epitaphs are not best written at a distance; the Castrol *Achievements* year book for 1937 said, *in memoriam*: '... Mr J. Guthrie was fatally injured on the Continent. He will always live in the minds of motorcyclists and in the hearts of his many friends, not only as a true sportsman with a delightful sense of humour, but as one of the greatest road-racing riders the world has ever known.'

The Entirely New Racing Mounts

The works' bikes for 1938 were considerably improved: they had to be if Norton were to stand any chance against their rivals' supercharged machinery. An engine redesign included new crankcases in lightweight Elektron magnesium alloy. The lower part of the cylinder barrel was deeply spigotted into the crankcases to increase rigidity and the cases themselves were finned in the fore-and-aft plane to aid cooling. The lower bevel box was reduced in size to enable the exhaust pipe to be tucked up out of the way, so improving ground clearance. The bore and stroke were altered – 82×94.3mm (498cc) and 75.9×77mm (348cc) – to reduce the piston speed and allow the engine to rev higher in safety. To take advantage of the higher revs, larger valves and a larger carburettor were used. The size of the megaphone on the exhaust was increased too, which aided top-end performance but made the engine more sensitive to valve and ignition timing; it also made it more 'peaky' (it had plenty of performance at the top end of the rev band but was much rougher in the low- to mid-range) which in turn made riding the bike harder work. The output of the 500cc engine was about 35bhp at 5,750rpm using a petrol/benzol mixture which gave the bike a top speed of around 125mph (200kph). The supercharged bikes, such as the BMW twin and the four-cylinder Gilera Rondine, were producing 15–20 horsepower more than the Norton and were around 20mph (30kph) faster.

Norton hoped that the superior handling and lighter weight of their bikes would make up for the power deficit. With this in mind an improved version of the plunger frame was produced. Although similar in appearance, the new frame used lighter, steel fittings instead of the heavy iron lugs which were traditionally used to join tubes and provide mountings. The L-shaped forgings that formed the lower frame cradle were replaced by tubes running from the front down-tube to the rear suspension mountings. The forged bridge-pieces which linked the top and bottom suspension mountings were also replaced by steel tubes. The plunger system itself was improved and

One of 'The Entirely New Racing Mounts' in the hands of Harold Daniell during the 1938 Senior TT. Daniell was an unlikely looking racer: short, fat, balding and short-sighted. Nevertheless he was a Grand Prix champion and he won the Senior TT in 1938 and 1949.

strengthened and the wheel-spindle clamps were made of alloy. A more radical change was the introduction of 'Roadholder' telescopic front forks. Similar to the forks which had been used by BMW for a number of years, the new forks were quite simple in construction: basically, each leg consisted of a pair of tubes, the lower tube sliding in a bush located in the upper tube; internal springs controlled both compression and rebound movement. On the BMW there was the sophistication of hydraulic damping and Norton led people to believe that this was a feature of their forks too. It was revealed some years later that this was not the case.

'The Entirely New Racing Mounts', as Norton called them, were ready just in time for the 1938 TT. Frith and White were joined by Harold Daniell, to form the official Norton team. The Junior race was won by Velocette, with Stanley Woods first and Ted Mellors second; the Norton men lined up in third, fourth and fifth places. Better things were expected in the Senior, where the BMW menace never really materialized: Karl Gall was injured in practice and Georg Meier had problems with a spark plug which put him out of the race within the first few minutes. That left Stanley Woods as Norton's main obstacle to another TT victory. Freddie Frith led the race for the first two laps before Woods got in front, the Norton team occupying the next three places. On the fifth lap Woods was only three seconds in front of Frith and Daniell. Frith broke the lap record (which he had set the year before) on this lap only to have Daniell break it again on the next lap. This put Daniell in the lead, a lead which he maintained despite both Woods and Frith lapping at over 90mph (145kph) on the last lap. Harold Daniell won by twelve seconds, his last lap at 91mph (145.6kph) a new record; Woods was second, Frith third.

A Change of Priorities

Norton failed to produce their usual run of success on the Continent in 1938. Daniell won both classes at the Swiss Grand Prix, but the blown BMWs proved to be too fast too often. In the 350cc class Nortons had a little more luck, picking up a couple of wins but the smaller engine failed to fulfil its promise (on a number of occasions the old single-cam engine had to be used). An unsatisfactory season and one which closed with the announcement that Norton would not be going racing in 1939. The reason, Norton stated, was that they had to concentrate on producing motorcycles for military contracts. The uneven struggle against the supercharged bikes was probably a contributory factor and the death of Jimmy Guthrie the previous year had also had

Harold Daniell on the Senior works' Norton in 1939. Winner of the 1938 Senior on 'The Entirely New Racing Mount', Daniell returned to the Island in 1939 with the works' bike but without factory support (busy with their military commitments). The race was dominated by the supercharged BMWs; Daniell retired with engine trouble.

Popping home for the weekend on the firm's bike. Flight Officer George Jaspis, a Belgian pilot in the RAF, uses his four days' leave (and the RAF's 16H) to visit his parents in Lille. The year is 1944 and his parents have not seen or heard of him in four years.

an effect upon the management. In January 1939 Joe Craig, mastermind of the racing programme, left to join BSA (to take charge of their intended racing effort), but he did not stay there long before moving on to a similar job at AJS. Joe Craig had been associated with Nortons since the mid-1920s, and his name had become inextricably linked with racing Nortons, but now Norton were racing no more. However, when Norton returned to the race-tracks Joe Craig returned to Norton.

There was no official Norton presence at the 1939 TT but the works' bikes were there, on loan to Daniell and Frith. Frith retired in the Junior and Daniell came second (behind Woods on a Velocette), despite a minor fall.

6

The WD 16H

Rugged, dependable and devoid of chrome plating, in its WD (War Department) guise, the 16H was an ideal dispatch rider's mount. Dull but dependable, it was a slow, heavy plodder that kept on going. The few faults it had were well known and unlikely to halt its progress totally: the rear wheel studs had a habit of coming loose, as did the magneto and its platform and the exposed gear-change linkage was prone to premature wear resulting in poor selection.

It was heavy – about 370lb (168kg) – and slow – flat out at 65mph (104kph) – and most dispatch riders quickly learnt to avoid soft sand or deep mud. The extra ground clearance provided by the trials-specification frame helped and the inherent rugged construction of the 16H meant that there was minimal damage when the bike did get dropped.

The WD 16H began production in 1938 and during the war years Norton introduced production-line methods to increase output. It is claimed that around 100,000 were produced but this may be war-time propaganda and an alternative figure of 60,000 is also mentioned.

The Senior race was a demonstration of BMW superiority: the supercharged twins were almost 30mph (48kph) faster than the Nortons. Meier and West took first and second, with Frith (now riding a Velocette) and Woods third and fourth respectively. Harold Daniell on the 1938 works' Norton retired with engine trouble.

Norton's decision to concentrate production on military contracts was a shrewd move. In the event of war, which was not certain at the end of 1938, it would keep them in the business of making motorcycles, something they did best (and was preferable to anonymous munitions manufacture). If war were avoided, they would at least have the military contracts, and the respite from racing would give them the time and the money to reconsider both their racing programme and their road bike range. With the exception of the International, Norton's range was a little staid. The recently introduced twin-cylinder Triumph and the acclaim it received suggested where the future might lie. However, it also emphasized the solid well-proven image of Norton's singles. It was this aspect that made them appealing to the military mind.

Despite denials that they were preparing for war, the Army had tested various motorcycles in the late 1930s. The standard issue BSA v-twin was just acceptable at the best of times but was unfit for service when the going got rough. The Army wanted something that was reliable, reasonably powerful and able to stand up to the kind of treatment it would receive from the British soldier. The 16H came out on top. Few modifications were needed to turn the 16H into a suitable war-machine. The only major difference between the standard 16H and the WD model was the use of the trials frame to provide extra ground clearance. The fitting of the trials bash-plate (to protect the crankcases) and the fork buffer-stops reduced the risk of damage over rough ground. The pre-1938-type cylinder barrel, with its pressed-steel valve cover, was retained for the WD model on the grounds that the later arrangement was an untried innovation. A cautious approach but, perhaps, a wise one. Uninspiring but adequate, the WD 16H earned an enviable reputation for reliability and was used in active service around the world.

Norton's other side-valve, the Big Four, also played a part in the war effort, although not to the same extent. In response to a War Office request, Norton produced a Big Four sidecar outfit with a driven sidecar wheel. The sidecar wheel was set back, in line with the bike's rear wheel, and drive was transmitted via a coupling on the rear axle. A dog-clutch allowed one- or two-wheel drive to be used as required (on hard surfaces the two-wheel drive, lacking a differential, made changing direction difficult). In skilled hands, the outfit could go almost anywhere – it had originally been devised, before the war, as a trials outfit and one was used as such by Dennis Mansell (the son of one of Norton's directors). The arrival of the American jeep killed the need for such a device and its production was dropped. A few survived the war and were sold off by the Army, generally with the sidecar-wheel drive crudely removed, but some survived (or were reconstructed) and are still in existence.

4

A Period of Transitions

'As You Were'

In September 1945, within months of the Second World War ending, Norton were back producing motorcycles for the public. Not unnaturally, production concentrated on a civilian version of the 16H and the Model 18, which shared many parts with the side-valve machine. The bikes were much as they had appeared before the war but both now used the cradle frame which had previously been specified on the ES2 and CS1 models. The 16H engine was fitted with enclosed valve-gear which had been introduced in 1938 but was not used for the military version. Both models were in short supply in Britain ('Export or die' urged the Labour government, a little dramatically) and subject to a heavy purchase tax. The 16H cost £99 (an increase of about 30 per cent on its pre-war price) plus £25 8s. 2d. tax and the Model 18 £105 plus £26 19s. tax. Still, personal transport was

The 16H was one of the first models to go back into production after the war. It was updated in 1948 but received little attention thereafter. Production of the 16H and Norton's other rigid-framed models ceased in 1954. This is one of the last of the line that began in Pa Norton's day.

scarce in the immediate post-war years and there were a large number of recently released military personnel eager to spend their demob gratuities.

Production of the 16H and Model 18 continued unchanged through 1946, but they were joined by two new models just in time for the Manx Grand Prix in September: the 30M and 40M Manx Grand Prix models. Norton had built a few racing Inters to special order before the war but now they were producing pure racers as catalogue models: not many, perhaps, and they were not available to just anyone (racing credentials required), but they were genuine production racers. They used the single overhead cam engine, more or less as seen in the 1936 works' models, in the plunger frame. Roadholder front forks were fitted and, unlike those used on the works' bikes before the war, they had the benefit of hydraulic damping. The Manx Grand Prix was the first major race held after the war and Norton produced the bikes to take advantage of the publicity it would receive. The Junior event was won by experienced Manx Grand Prix rider Ken Bills, riding one of the new production racers – five out of the first six bikes were Nortons; the Senior race, however, was won by Ernie Lyons, riding a Triumph twin. Bills and his Norton came second.

More models became available in 1947. The ES2 returned (basically a Model 18 engine in a plunger frame) and so did the Big Four. The old side-valve (Pa Norton's Model 1) used the improved cylinder head which had been developed for the military outfit, giving it a little more power. The Inter, in both 350 and 500 form, also reappeared, the first one off the production line going to George Formby, comedian, singer, film star and keen motorcyclist. He received the Inter at a special presentation at the Norton factory following a

BBC radio broadcast there. In fact, he had had the bike for a while, but it was good publicity.

Comings and Goings

All the 1947 models were fitted with Roadholder telescopic forks, incorporating a speedometer mounting in the top fork yoke and hydraulic damping. Although most manufacturers were beginning to fit telescopic forks, they were not greeted with enthusiasm by all motorcyclists of the period (conservative as ever) but, as the manufacturers were quick to point out, 'teles' were superior: after all, they were used for racing. They were also cheaper to produce.

Bill Mansell, Norton's Managing Director for twenty years, left the company in 1947. He had been with the company since 1913 when it had been bought by R T Shelley. His son Dennis, a director since 1938 also left with him. Dennis had a long history of trials success with Norton outfits and had helped develop the two-wheel-drive sidecar outfit for military use. They both had business interests elsewhere, notably the engineering company Abingdon King Dick, the company that supplied Norton's oil pumps. Their places on the board were taken by men with familiar names: E R (Reg) Shelley and G A (Tony) Vandervell, both sons of Norton directors. Joe Craig, another familiar name, returned to run the racing department. He had spent eight years as chief designer and development engineer with AMC, working on their blown v-four and the equally troublesome 'Porcupine' twin. His dislike of multi-cylinder engines was probably reinforced by this period. At Norton he was employed as Engineering Director, with responsibility for engineering and technical development, but of course his racing interests took preference.

The side- and overhead valve engines were updated in 1948; externally little seemed to change but, actually, there were few components carried over from the old design. This turned out to be the last time that the 'underhead cam' singles received any real attention from the design office. Any future improvements these models received were incidental, the company's interests being elsewhere. The old hinged cam-followers were replaced by simpler, sliding tappets (which, on the side-valve engines, incorporated adjusters and worked directly on to the valves). This allowed a reduction in size of the timing case, although its shape changed very little. The cylinder barrel on the side-valves was simplified by the introduction of a separate cast-alloy valve chamber (known as a 'chimney pot', from its shape) which was inserted between the cylinder and crankcases. An oblong cover, held by a single screw, gave access to the valves. The chamber also incorporated the exhaust valve lifter. Cast-alloy cylinder heads were also new to the side-valve models. The stroke of the Big Four was reduced from 120mm to 113mm, reducing its capacity to 597cc and breaking a direct link with the first Big Four designed by James Norton himself in 1907. Both types of engine began to use smaller diameter flywheels which allowed pistons with longer skirts to be fitted (this helped to reduce piston slap and so reduce engine noise). The overhead valve engines also received a new, one-piece rocker-box with improved lubrication and valve gear.

Strangers in the Camp

Any impact the updated 1948 singles might have had was reduced by the arrival that year of a new and – for Norton – unusual model: a twin. In some ways it was not a totally unexpected move but it did not fit easily into the Norton range. The arrival of the parallel twin as the standard engine in British motorcycling began really with Triumph in 1937. Their Speed Twin proved popular enough to persuade other manufacturers that they had to follow suit. The war intervened before any of them could go into production but within a few years of it ending most of the manufacturers had their own design of parallel twin either in, or nearing production. Norton's Chief Draughtsman, Edgar Franks, had proposed an in-line twin but the management, playing safe, wanted something more like the

Tony Vandervell tries out Harold Daniell's 1947 TT-winner; Norton's Managing Director Gilbert Smith stands by approvingly. The 'fish-tail' on the end of the exhaust was an attempt to keep the bike within the realms of decency; the substantial bracketry was an attempt to keep the exhaust on the bike – vibration was a problem.

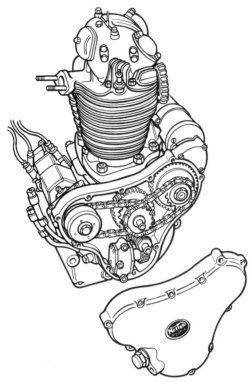

Norton's First Parallel Twin. Carefully designed to be similar to, but not the same as, Triumph's twin, the Model 7 Dominator engine and its derivatives stayed in production much longer than was expected. It is seen here in its earliest form with cast-iron cylinder head and integral inlet manifold.

Bert Hopwood, who was appointed chief draugtsman in 1947 and was responsible for the Dominator engine. Disagreement with Joe Craig forced Hopwood's departure almost as soon as the twin was finished. Hopwood returned in 1955 (the year in which Craig retired) only to encounter problems from another, more unexpected quarter.

Triumph engine. Another draughtsman, Jack Moore, produced a second design to meet this requirement, but this too was rejected. It was decided instead that a 'hired hand' would be brought in to design the new engine: someone with experience of 'multis'.

The man chosen by Gilbert Smith was Bert Hopwood, who had worked on twins and fours for Triumph and Ariel. Hopwood was given a blank sheet of paper and told to produce a design for a twin. However, Norton had neither the budget nor the facilities to produce the engine Hopwood considered ideal, so his

eventual design was a compromise. Despite this, it became a popular and very long-running design.

Most of the other companies that produced twin-cylinder motorcycles sold them as the top of their particular range. The Twin was, or quickly became, the largest-engined, the quickest and the most expensive bike in a manufacturer's catalogue. Not so with Norton. At its introduction in 1948, the new Model 7 was priced at £216; the Inter at that time cost £247 and the competition-only Manx was £314. Norton's fame had been built on the success of the cammy racers and the Inter was so closely associated with them as to be almost indistinguishable. Even if the Norton twin had any real racing potential, it would need plenty of development and, anyway, it did not have the mystique that was attached to the overhead cam single. The twin had to play second fiddle to the Inter. The chief reason for the continued existence of the Inter, which only sold in small numbers after the war, was its direct association with the works' racers. The racing department had become a *raison d'être* for the rest of the company and far too much time, effort and money was spent on keeping the Manx competitive.

The twin was at a disadvantage from the beginning for a number of other reasons too. Norton were not a large, wealthy company despite the WD contracts that had sustained them during the war. As they approached the 1950s they were still little more than an assembler of motorcycles (with most of the components coming from the Vandervell/ Shelley family of companies) much as they had been in Pa Norton's day. In a good week Norton might produce two hundred bikes, while Triumph and BSA would each produce

Bert Hopwood's twin-cylinder engine as it appeared in the Model 7. The engine was a compromise but that's what engineering is all about. Still, it was a successful compromise – how much more successful could Bert Hopwood's preferred design have been?

Norton used their racing pedigree as a point in the Dominator's favour. In fact, the twin gained little from the factory's racing programme and there was mutual antipathy between its designer Bert Hopwood and the race chief Joe Craig.

five or six times that number. Low-volume production prevented cheaper production methods, such as die-casting, from being used at Norton. The cylinder head for the twin had to be sand-cast because it was produced in relatively small numbers. Sand-casting also influenced its design, resulting in the need for a series of time-consuming and difficult machining operations.

Also, Norton's machine tools were past their best, having been just about worn out meeting the military contracts. Norton did not have the equipment to make a sophisticated new engine. They could not afford to design, develop and build a truly high quality twin; their twin had to be built down to a price, if they were going to be able to produce one at all. The Inter, on the other hand, had never

been constrained by financial considerations: it had always been the direct beneficiary of the all-important racer's development programme. Added to this were Norton's semi-secret plans to produce a four-cylinder racer. They were involved with BRM in the development of a four which would replace the single as the works' racer. Norton were certainly not a large enough company to spend time and money on the single, the twin and the four. The single was well established, the four was the (possible) future and the twin was, perhaps, a necessary evil: everyone else was making them, so Norton felt obliged to produce one.

Initially, there were few friends for the twin at Norton. The company had become famous for their singles and the pervading attitude

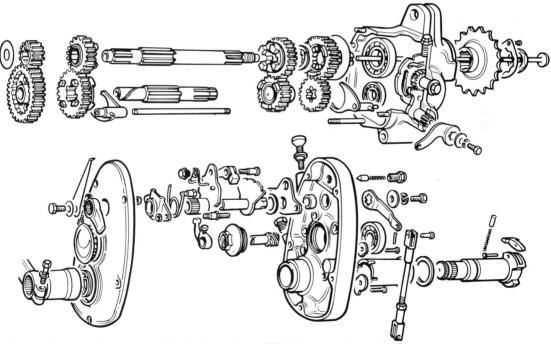

Norton's four-speed gearbox as fitted to the post-war ES2. Norton took over the Sturmey Archer gearbox in 1934 and developed it gradually over the years. This version has the positive-stop mechanism integral to the main gearbox housing; it evolved into the 'laid down' type which was fitted to the Dominator and later models.

was conservative, to say the least. There was also direct antipathy from Joe Craig who had not got on well with Hopwood and had felt threatened by his proposals for Norton's future (Hopwood was no lover of racing, preferring development to be concentrated on production motorcycles) Craig was responsible for production of the twin being delayed while he examined possible means of improving its power output. No improvements were needed and none were introduced, but the engine's production was held up needlessly for a few weeks. That it continued in production and later became as successful as it did

The Model 7 used the ES2 frame and cycle parts but the petrol tank and mudguards were unique to the twin. The 'laid-down' gearbox was introduced on the Model 7. The dual saddle was not original but could be bought as an accessory at the time.

was due to a fortunate combination of circumstances, and then to a triumph of development over design.

The Model 7

The twin-cylinder engine first appeared in the Model 7. The Model 7 used the same cycle parts as the ES2: plunger frame, Roadholder telescopic forks, 21-inch front wheel, 19-inch rear wheel and 7-inch brakes on both. However, it used a new variation of the Sturmey Archer/Norton gearbox. The upper, bifurcated lug (which, if loose, quickly became worn and was then easily broken) was replaced by a solid lug. The positive-stop mechanism was moved from the top of the gearbox to a position in front of the kickstart. This improved the gear selection linkage and reduced the gearbox's overall height. In this form, it became known as the 'laid-down' gearbox and was used, in one form or another, into the 1970s.

The petrol tank was chrome-plated, with panels in Norton's traditional silver with black and red lining. Inserted into the tank to the left of the filler cap was an oil-pressure gauge. The speedometer was housed in the top fork yoke. The only other instrument fitted was an ammeter, located in the headlamp shell. Rider comfort was provided by a sprung saddle but there was little consideration given to the passenger: an optional pad could be fitted on to the rear mudguard, with the footrests (another option) sited awkwardly high and too far to the rear. Sidecar fixing lugs were a standard feature.

Although the Model 7 was exhibited at the Earls Court Show in November, 1948, the bike was not immediately available to the British public. The first consideration was the export market, so it was well into the follow-

The Dominator

Norton called the new twin the Model 7 when it was first announced, towards the end of 1948, but it soon acquired the name 'Dominator'. The name was carried on throughout the bike's development, into the 1960s. It was designed by Bert Hopwood, with assistance from Jack Moore, Doug Hele and Bill Pitcher. A number of factors dictated its basic design: chiefly that it had to be similar to, but not the same as, the successful Triumph engine; it had to be reasonably cheap and easy to produce; and it had to be a 360-degree twin. This latter parameter was allegedly due to the design of British magnetos available at the time (a case of the tail wagging the dog?).

The crankcases were split vertically with an equal-size bearing in each half supporting the crankshafts. The crankshaft was a three-piece affair with a central flywheel bolted between two forged bobweights which incorporated the crankshafts and the big-end bearings. Split connecting rods with shell-bearings were used. The right crankcase-half formed the inner part of the timing chest. The timing-side shaft carried a small pinion and was secured by a nut with a drive-worm. This worm drove the gear-type oil pump (designed by Franks and used by Norton since 1930). The timing-shaft pinion drove an intermediate gear which carried two sprockets: one sprocket drove the single camshaft at the front of the engine and the other drove the magneto at the rear of the engine. A fibre gear on the camshaft worked through an inertia clutch to drive the external dynamo.

Phosphor bronze bushes in the crankcases carried the camshaft, which worked upon the tappets located in the cylinder barrel. Alloy push-rods ran within the barrel casting, up to the one-piece cylinder head. The cast-iron barrel was spigotted into the crankcases and bolted to them through a flange. The cylinder head (cast-iron on early engines, alloy from 1955 onwards) had two widely splayed exhaust ports and, on early engines only, one inlet port. Later engines had two ports with a detachable siamesed inlet port (and even later engines used two carburettors on separate tracts). The rocker-box was V-shaped, its apex at the rear of the engine. The rocker-shafts originally had flanges by which they were bolted to the head, but later shafts were simple rods, retained by flat plates.

The bore and stroke of the Model 7 was 66×72.6mm, giving a capacity of 497cc. The compression ratio was 6.7:1, which was quite low, but it had to be to deal with the low-octane petrol of the time. Nevertheless, the early Model 7 produced 29bhp at 6,000rpm. This was good enough to give the bike a top speed of around 90mph (145kph) with, for the time, good acceleration. This was comparable with the top speed of the Inter of the period.

Despite the constraints (financial and other) placed upon them, Hopwood's team designed a competent unit, no worse than most others of the time, and superior to many. It was improved in later years and became the match of the Triumph twin. Unfortunately, it was stretched beyond its limits in the 1960s and lost much of its reliability and pleasantness. But that could be said of much of the motorcycle industry.

ing year before the Norton twin was seen on the road in Britain. When the motorcycle press did get their hands on one, it received favourable comments (although it should be said that the motorcycle press of the period were not noted for their forthright criticism – as long as a bike had an engine that would run and wheels that were round they would think of something nice to say about it). The Model 7's performance was up to that of the Inter and some suggested it was even superior. Top speed was around 90mph (145kph) and the twin-cylinder engine was more flexible than the cammy single. It had the twin's usual virtues of easy starting and good acceleration, and the usual vice of vibration was not too apparent. The handling was good but it was achieved partly by using stiff suspension, a feature which added to rider discomfort. The brakes received some criticism but it is possible that the lack of engine braking, compared with that available from a single, may have been a factor. There was one area where the Model 7 was undoubtedly superior to the Inter: oil retention. The Model 7's valves and valve-gear were totally enclosed; even when ridden hard it did not leak oil. Given the same treatment, the Inter, with its exposed valves, would waterproof its rider's flannels!

The 500T

Another new model exhibited at the 1948 Show was the 500T. This was a trials model using a 500cc overhead valve engine in a modified 16H frame. Since the war, Norton had been offering, to special order, a trials bike using an iron engine in a 16H frame, but the new bike was offered as a production model. The engine was based on the ES2 but had an alloy head and alloy barrel. The frame was a shortened version of the WD 16H (53-inch instead of 56-inch) and used Roadholder teles with different fork yokes to give the required trials steering geometry. The frame only just accommodated the overhead valve engine but it did provide a worthwhile 7½-inch ground clearance (standard road models had about 4 inches). (It is interesting to note that rigid frames were considered essential for trials bikes in those days; a sprung frame, it was believed, would just bounce around on rough terrain and prevent the wheel from transmitting the drive.) The trials specification included a bash-plate to protect the underside of the engine, alloy engine plates and mudguards, alloy front brake-plate (and lightened drum) and a lightweight 2½-gallon

Geoff Godber-Ford powering the 500T to a first-class award in the Manville Cup Trial in 1951. He was one of the leading trials riders of the day and part of Norton's official team from 1945–51.

(11.5-litre) petrol tank. The weight-saving exercise produced a bike which weighed about 320lb (145kg), almost 50lb (23kg) less than a comparable road bike. The 500T was a competent trials bike and earned a good reputation but Norton failed to develop the idea and other, more specialized bikes made it obsolete. The 500T sold for £177 3s. 4d. on its introduction in 1948, slightly less than the ES2: an unusual instance of a specialized competition bike costing less than a standard road model. Manufacturers nowadays don't make that kind of mistake.

The 500T

Norton had a long tradition of offering their bikes in trials specification, but it wasn't until 1949 that they produced a purpose-built trials model, the 500T. The 500T was the result of two years hybridization using standard Norton parts to produce a specialist trials bike.

The Model 18 formed the basis for Norton's first post-war trials machine but it was not an entirely successful attempt. At 370lb (168kg) it was overweight and when telescopic forks were added (without altering the steering head angle) it became almost unrideable. The 500T had redesigned steering geometry and a short-wheelbased frame based on the WD 16H frame (rigid frames were still considered necessary for trials bikes) which improved matters greatly. Further improvements came from the use of lighter cycle parts and the introduction of an alloy version of the overhead valve engine. The absence of lights and the dynamo helped to further reduce weight. In this form the 500T weighed about 50lb (22kg) less than the Model 18.

The 500T proved to be a competent trials machine and was used at all levels of the sport. It received a few, minor modifications during its production run but was dropped from the range in 1954 following Norton's takeover by AMC.

Back on the Track

Norton's cammy singles had dominated the 1930s' racing scene until the arrival of the supercharged multi. In 1946, when international race meetings once again became a possibility, it was decided that supercharging would be banned. This brought Norton back to the tracks and Joe Craig back to Norton. The new regulations stipulated that the standard, commercially available petrol of the period must be used. This was poor quality stuff compared with the special fuels permitted before the war, but it was a problem for everyone. As Norton had not become involved with supercharging, they had something of an advantage over their rivals: they did not have to develop a new engine or modify one that had been designed for supercharging. A reprieve, but for how long?

The 1947 TT gave Norton some hope, but it showed that they were not the only ones to benefit from the ban. Velocettes took the first four places in the Junior race and gave Norton a hard time in the Senior event. However it was a Norton victory, with Harold Daniell and TT newcomer Artie Bell bringing their works' bikes home first and second.

With little time to prepare for the 1947 TT, Joe Craig had been forced to use the 1938 works' bikes suitably modified. For the following year, when things were not so rushed,

Sand in the Works

In many ways the annual Daytona Beach Races were the equivalent of the Isle of Man TT for the American bike enthusiast. Daytona was the single most important event in the American bike racing calendar. The main event was the 200 Mile Experts' Race. This was run on a 4.1 mile (6.56km) track which consisted of a 2-mile (3.2km) straight on the beach and a similar straight on an adjacent road linked by a pair of banked curves. The event was traditionally won by Indian or Harley, but in 1941 Bill Matthews upset the equilibrium by winning on a cammy Norton 500.

After the war, Gilbert Smith decided to enter a couple of works' bikes at the suggestion of the North American importer, Bill McGill. McGill had prepared Matthews' winning bike in 1941 and his son was serving an apprenticeship at Bracebridge Street. They knew the value of a win at Daytona and its effect on sales. In 1948, Smith sent Steve Lancefield to oversee the operation on Norton's behalf. Despite having been forewarned by McGill about the peculiar requirements of Daytona Lancefield was not fully prepared for the event. However, Bill Matthews did come second riding the works' Norton and may even have won the race but the scorers were unsure about the exact order of the finishers. Being patriotic, they decided in favour of the Indian rider Floyd Emde.

In 1949 Gilbert Smith asked Francis Beart to organize the works' entry at Daytona. Beart was one of the top Norton tuners and had a perfectionist approach to bike preparation. He also had the benefit of Lancefield's experience. His preparation and organization were faultless: the works' bikes ridden by Dick Klamforth, Bill Matthews and Tex Luse came first, second and third. Beart had enabled Norton to beat Indian and Harley-Davidson on their home ground and in a convincing fashion. Francis Beart returned to Daytona in 1950 and 1951 and provided the factory with success on both occasions (Matthews won in 1951 and Klamforth in 1952).

In 1949, the Indian Sales Corporation had taken over Norton distribution in America and for 1952 they handled the Norton entry at Daytona. Dick Klamforth won again. It was good publicity for Norton but it proved too much for Harley-Davidson. They pushed the American Motorcycle Association – the controlling body for motorcycle sport in America – into banning overhead cam engines. Five race-prepared Dominator twins were entered with factory backing in 1953 and one managed to come fourth. Norton showed less interest in racing the twins and the Harley 750cc side-valves had too much of an advantage. Norton sales in America were further affected in 1953 following their take-over by AMC and by Indian's own financial problems which reduced their effectiveness as an importer. Norton made a serious attempt at Daytona in 1964, with a handful of Domiracers prepared by Francis Beart and Paul Dunstall but with no success. They tried again nearly ten years later with the John Player Commandos but they never did repeat the victories of the early 1950s.

Norton-mounted Don Evans executes a less than perfect broadside at the end of the 1950 Daytona Amateur race. He nearly executed the man with the flag, too.

Norton's successful team for the 1950 Daytona beach race. The riders are: winner Bill Mathews (98); second-placed Dick Klamforth (2), the previous year's winner; and fourth man Bill Tuman. Francis Beart stands between Mathews and Klamforth.

a number of changes were introduced: stiffer crankcases (common to both the 350 and 500 for the first time) with altered mountings, hydraulic damping on the rear suspension, 19-inch rear wheel, shorter front forks and twin-leading-shoe brakes, plus a host of other detail changes. Not all the improvements were apparent: the linkage for the twin-leading-shoe brakes was concealed inside the brake-plates, making them more complicated than was necessary. However, this hid the nature of the brakes from the opposition, and gave the Norton team a psychological advantage.

There must have been an advantage of one kind or another that year, for Nortons won the Senior TT with a hat-trick: Artie Bell, Bill Doran and Jock Weddell, in that order. The Junior TT went to Velocette once again.

The ban on supercharging had benefited the Norton singles to a certain extent but it was a short-term benefit. The continental factories were working on bikes that would be more than a match for the old cammy Norton:

In the late forties and fifties Manx Norton engines became popular in Formula 3 car racing. Perversely, Norton were not pleased with this and refused to supply engines for such use. This resulted in complete bikes being bought and then dumped after their engines and gearboxes had been extracted. This double overhead cam engine is installed in a car which was built by Mike Erskine and raced in the early fifties.

Gilera's four weighed less than the Norton and produced more power, but had suffered from handling and reliability problems; Moto Guzzi's twin had shown itself the match of the Norton, but also suffered reliability problems; and a small company called MV Agusta were also working on a four-cylinder design. Joe Craig appreciated the threat from the AJS 'Porcupine' twin (he had worked for AJS during the war years), and there was a rumour that Velocette were working on a four . . .

The Way Ahead?

Norton's Managing Director, Gilbert Smith, understood the problem and was organizing a solution: Norton were to race a four of their own. The engine would be developed in conjunction with British Racing Motors, who were working on a V16-engined racing car. BRM was a peculiar organization, set up to take advantage of the various fields of expertise in the motoring industry, the companies involved providing finance and any particular specialist expertise that was required. In 1948, Norton signed a contract with BRM which would provide them with the design for a four-cylinder engine based on the V16. Through R.T. Shelley Ltd, Norton agreed to pay £750 per annum which would allow them to take advantage of developments arising from BRM's research. Norton also provided the services of Joe Craig, to advise on cams, cylinder head design, etc. One of Norton's directors Tony Vandervell (son of Norton's chairman C A Vandervell) was also involved in his capacity as a specialist bearing manufacturer. In fact it was at his suggestion that Norton became involved in the project.

Unfortunately, there were problems even before the agreement was signed. Norton's link with BRM, Peter Berthon, was somewhat ineffectual and put little effort into the four-cylinder engine. Norton's interests were continually ignored or postponed. To make matters worse, Tony Vandervell and BRM's boss, Raymond Mays, did not see eye-to-eye on many things. Vandervell was incisive, knowledgeable and blunt, and he believed that even if Mays knew what he wanted, he did not know how to get it. Vandervell pulled out of the BRM organization in 1950 to run his own racing car project. He went on to develop his own Formula One car, ironically using a four-cylinder engine closely based on the Manx design. He also developed something of a vendetta against Mays and was pleased to see his own car, the Vanwall, go on to glory while the BRM never really fulfilled its promise.

Despite these set-backs, a single-cylinder unit was built during 1953 using the dimensions from the four. It was a test-rig unit and never intended to be installed in a motorcycle frame. It produced almost 12bhp and ran to 13,000 rpm, indicating a potential of around 50bhp for the four (the works' 500cc single that year was producing about 40bhp). There is a rumour that a four-cylinder engine was track-tested but it is unlikely that it was the BRM–derived unit (it may have been the prototype double overhead cam four built by JAP). Ultimately, nothing came of the Norton four. The involvement with BRM had done Norton no good and wasted a lot of Joe Craig's time.

The decision to get involved with a four-cylinder engine had been questionable from the start and was one which Gilbert Smith himself soon regretted. Norton did not have the money required to perfect a four and they certainly could not have made a production version. Joe Craig was, perhaps, not the right man for the job either. He was a confirmed 'singles man' for a start. He knew his Nortons, but his knowledge had been empirically

Norton's World Sidecar Championships

Norton-powered sidecar outfits were successful in trials and road-racing in the 1930s, and Norton produced a handful of 600cc overhead cam engines specifically for such use. The majority of these used single cam cylinder heads but a few twin cam engines were also produced. When the first World Sidecar Championship series was run, in 1949, it was won with a 600cc single overhead cam Norton engine.

The winner of the first championship was an Englishman, Eric Oliver, with the now-famous motoring journalist Dennis Jenkinson as his passenger. Oliver raced for fun – there was little money to be won and he subsidized his sidecar racing by also riding in solo events, which paid better. Although he won four World Championships using Norton engines, the support Oliver received from the factory was minimal: 'Norton presented me with a clock – I think they'd been given it by Smiths – and loaned me an engine for winning the first championship. The second time I did it I was awarded an attaché case. I got nothing for the next two titles.' This, despite the fact that Gilera had offered him £500 to use their engines (which were also more powerful than Norton's).

Oliver did receive assistance from Ron Watson of Watsonian Sidecars who recognized the promotional value of the championship series. Oliver won the championship three years in succession (1949–51) with a rigid-framed, girder-forked Norton. His passenger in 1950 and 1951 was Lorenzo Dobelli – an Italian who couldn't speak a word of English. The sidecar was a simple platform bolted on to the standard Norton frame in the manner of a conventional outfit. Oliver broke a leg in 1952, which put him out of the championship, but the series was still won by an Englishman – Cyril Smith. Smith also rode a Norton but his outfit was more specialized. It was lower and used a purpose-built frame and benefited from a comprehensive fairing. Oliver, with Stan Dibben passengering, campaigned a similar outfit to win the championship in 1953. He was favourite to win in 1954 too, but broke his arm before the Swiss Grand Prix. He had it wired up so that he could still compete, but spun the outfit in the wet during the race and re-broke the arm. He carried on racing, to finish fifth but it was not quite enough. The Championship went to Willie Noll riding a BMW. The German flat-twin engine had taken over from the Gilera as the Norton's main challenger.

Oliver officially retired in 1954 and the World Sidecar Championship was not won by a Briton again for twenty-five years. BMW-powered outfits dominated the sport during that time. Norton outfits continued to figure in the results during the 1950s and even into the 1960s, driven by Cyril Smith, Bill Boddice, Pip Harris and Jackie Beeton, but they appeared with less frequency. Eric Oliver reappeared for a special performance in the 1958 Sidecar TT. He drove a standard Norton Dominator fitted with a Watsonian Monaco sports sidecar, passengered by Mrs Pat Wise. The outfit was a conventional road-going combination and probably 30mph (48kph) slower than the race-winner's BMW. Still, Oliver's lap times were only 4mph (6.5kph) slower and he managed to finish in tenth place. Not bad for a same-as-you-can-buy outfit. James Norton would have been proud.

gained over the years. He did not have the theoretical ability to develop a four. However, he was the Technical Director, so it was his responsibility. His main concern, running the race team, was given to ace Norton-tuner Steve Lancefield during 1949, in order to give Craig the time to work on the four, but in fact, Joe Craig spent little of that year working with BRM. Apart from the fact that BRM was dreadfully inefficient and slow, Craig had personal preoccupations: he was involved in a car crash that year and another accident, on his motorcycle, had caused the death of his wife. The development of an unwanted and (to Craig) unnecessary four was of little importance.

Eric Oliver and Les Nutt with their full-faired Norton outfit (styling by Dan Dare) in 1954. Oliver won Grands Prix events at the Isle of Man, Ulster and Belgium that year and came fifth in the Swiss GP (with a broken arm), but it was not enough to give him the world title. BMW's domination had begun and Oliver retired, aged forty-four.

No luxury race transporter for the 1952 World Sidecar Champion. Cyril Smith picks up his racing outfit from the Reynolds factory. Smith worked for Norton but any assistance he received was unofficial. Even as late as 1952 Smith still preferred to race a rigid-framed outfit.

Non-standard Manx prepared by Francis Beart during the late forties. The reinforcing gussets on the rear frame were a feature which the factory planned to copy for the 1950 season: they were saved the bother by the arrival of the Featherbed frame.

Rising Stars

The 1949 season, however, emphasized the need for Norton to produce something special if they were to remain competitive. That year the World Championship series was instituted. It was won by Les Graham on the AJS twin. Graham very nearly won the Senior TT too, but his magneto failed on the last lap and Harold Daniell picked up first place for Norton. Velocette continued their run of luck, winning the Junior TT and the 350cc class of the World Championship. Norton had more success later in the year at the Manx Grand Prix. One of their works' trials riders displayed his ability on the track and won the Senior Clubman's TT and the Senior Manx

Grand Prix. His name was Geoff Duke. (During his military service in the Royal Signals Corps Duke had received training as a dispatch rider. Two of the men who had trained him were, perhaps, a little over-qualified: ex-works' Norton riders Crasher White and Freddie Frith.)

Norton had steadily developed the 'Manx' engine for nearly twenty years. Despite the poor quality post-war fuel, its power output had increased by 30 per cent in that time. The performance of the tyres and the brakes had also been improved, but the bike's handling was lagging behind. The frame was heavy and becoming increasingly prone to breaking. The plunger suspension was inadequate and, as engine performance and top speeds increased, probably caused more problems than it had originally solved. The racing Norton of the late 1940s was a big, heavy motorcycle that needed a brave, determined rider if it were to perform well; even then, it was a handful.

A Famous Frame

All this changed in 1950. Norton were presented with a ready-made solution to the handling problem. Works rider Artie Bell had experimented with frame and rear suspension during most of the 1940s, in partnership with the McCandless brothers, Rex and Cromie. Rex had designed and built a number of racing

specials and produced kits to convert rigid frames to swinging-arm suspension. Bell's link with Norton led to the trio producing a new frame for the Manx engine. It was more successful than either party could have imagined and significantly increased the engine's competitive life.

The new frame was an all-welded, tubular affair, without forgings or castings to add unnecessary weight. The main frame section consisted of a double loop which formed an open-box arrangement around the engine and gearbox. On each side, a frame tube ran from the top of the steering head, down under the engine, curved behind the gearbox to run up to the rear of the petrol tank and curved again to run back towards the steering head. At the

The product of the McCandless brothers and using aircraft technology, the Featherbed frame enabled Norton to remain competitive in post-war racing. The frame gave Norton's production bikes a competitive edge and went on to become 'the frame that launched a thousand specials'.

The Featherbed Frame

The Featherbed frame was the answer to Joe Craig's prayers in 1949. The works racers were becoming uncompetitive against the European multis in Grand Prix racing – the Nortons were underpowered and frame breakages were a recurring problem. The solution was supplied by Ulster engineer Rex McCandless. A specialist in frame design, he supplied Norton with a ready-to-race replacement for the heavy and ill-handling Gardengate frame. The Featherbed frame was both lighter and stronger than its predecessor and provided handling which was to set the standard for almost twenty years. McCandless also produced a prototype frame for the Dominator, which used a stressed-skin monocoque rear assembly, but Norton chose to play safe and used the Featherbed with its more conventional appearance.

front of the petrol tank the tube was kinked inwards to meet up with the bottom of the steering head; just before this junction the top frame run contacted the down-tube and they were welded together at this point. A cross-member was used to brace the top tube at the point where it kinked. The two sides of the frame were mirror-images of each other. The frame curve at the back of the gearbox was gussetted for extra strength and to provide a bracket to attach the tubular swinging arm. At the base of the gusset another cross-member added to the frame's integrity and provided a mounting for the gearbox. A light triangulated framework bolted on to the rear of the frame to support the rider and provide a top mounting for the rear suspension units (after 1950 this sub-frame was welded on).

The new frame used a shortened version of the Roadholder forks, with two-way hydraulic damping. The centre of gravity of the bike was further reduced by the use of 19-inch wheels front and rear. The rear wheel travel was controlled by a pair of suspension units which featured hydraulic dampers with external reservoirs. A large slab-sided petrol tank sat on the top tubes, insulated by rubber padding, and held down by a central strap. It contained nearly 6 gallons (27 litres), ideal for long-distance races such as the TT (a smaller tank, for short-circuit races, was later pro-

duced). An angular, alloy oil tank with an 8-pint (4.5-litre) capacity was mounted centrally above the gearbox. The difference between the old and the new frames was encapsulated by Harold Daniell, a man who had fought the plunger frame round the Island faster than anyone else: on trying out the new frame for the first time, he declared that it was 'like a bloody featherbed' in comparison. And that, suitably disencarnadined, is how it became known.

Off-season developments led to the production of new crankcases and a new cambox in an attempt to reduce any chance of misalignment of engine internals and reduce vibration. The bimetallic head was replaced by an all-alloy head with valve seat inserts, and the top of the vertical cam-drive shaft became enclosed by the cylinder head fins. Matters were further improved with the introduction of higher grade (80 octane) petrol.

The new bike had its first competitive outing, with Geoff Duke riding, at the Blandford circuit at the start of the season. The result, an overwhelming success, is part of the Norton enthusiast's litany. As is the result of that year's TT: Bell, Duke, Daniell and Lockett came first, second, third and sixth in the Junior; and Duke, Bell, Lockett and Daniell were first, second, third and fifth in the Senior. In the Senior, Duke set a new lap

Harold Daniell's Senior TT Norton. The Featherbed frame was good enough to give Norton a TT double in its first year (1950). The rear sub-frame (detachable on the earliest examples) was welded up at the end of the first season and the angle of the suspension units was changed but that was all. A testimony to Rex McCandless's abilities.

record of 93.33mph (150.2kph), breaking the lap record of 91mph (146.4kph) set by Daniell twelve years earlier. Interestingly, eighth place in both races went to a man who had been partly responsible for Norton's victories, Cromie McCandless. He too rode a Norton (prepared by top Norton tuner Francis Beart), but not one of the new breed; he had had to make do with the old 'Gardengate' model.

Production Frames

The more mundane singles of the Norton range were neglected after the update they had received in 1948. Norton's resources were spread thinly during that period and any changes meant extra expenditure, a thing to be avoided. Nevertheless, the side-valve and overhead valve range received the laid-down gearbox in 1950. This simplified production, as the gearbox was already used on the Model 7 and was to be used on production versions of the Manx. There was little changed over the next two years, but a swinging-arm frame for the ES2 was announced late in 1952. Unfortunately it was not the Featherbed frame, although the Featherbed frame had had a part in its production. Much was made of the improvement in handling that the new frame had brought to the racers and in 1951 an 'export only' version of the twin-engine in the Featherbed frame had been released. This was the Dominator De-Luxe, the Model 88. As the Inters were also to receive the Featherbed frame, the overhead valve singles were left looking like the poor relations in the Norton family. Even if the side-valve models had no sporting pretensions, the plunger frame was causing lost sales for the ES2 (if any one factor was responsible) and also the Model 7.

Unfortunately, there were not enough Featherbed frames to go round. The frame was made for Norton by the Reynolds Tube Company and they were having difficulty supplying enough frames for the Dominator De-

Luxe and the cammy singles. So Norton came up with a variation of the old cradle frame with a grafted-on swinging arm. This was not as good as the Featherbed but still an improvement. The swinging arm ES2 and Model 7 were introduced for 1953.

Frame Production

It was not widely known at the time that the Featherbed frames were not made by Norton. The first few had been made by Rex McCandless and ace welder Olly Nelson. When Norton wanted the frame produced in large numbers they approached Reynolds,

The ES2 received a swinging arm frame (hurriedly constructed by Bob Collier) in 1953. It was an improvement but the singles went on the decline following the introduction of the Dominator. This well-restored 1954 example has some non-original items but is no less appealing.

Rex McCandless produced this prototype of a Featherbed-framed Dominator but it was considered too extreme by the conservative Norton management (although they did adopt the curious front mudguard arrangement). The front part of the frame uses the standard Featherbed design but the rear is a stressed skin construction.

who were leaders in welded assemblies and tube technology. At the time, all-welded frames were an advanced idea, one which even twenty years later had not been adopted by all manufacturers. Reynolds agreed to make the frames and from 1951 onwards made them all. The works' bikes used top-grade 531 tubing, as did the production Manx frames (apart from a very small number of the earliest frames). The Inters used A-quality mild steel and the frames for the twins were made from B-quality tubing. In taking on the work, Reynolds had been forced to keep their involvement secret. They needed the business and Norton wanted the glory. The arrangement worked to Norton's advantage and did much for their reputation.

Motorcycle sales had increased rapidly since the end of the war but Norton had not benefited as much as other companies. They had been a bit slow off the mark with the Dominator and, initially anyway, this did not have the image or reputation that the Triumph had acquired. Also, too much effort had been put into improving the Manx. Although this had had the desired effect of enabling Norton to win races, it backfired on them: the Manx engine made the other singles look hopelessly dated and the new Featherbed frame showed up the shortcomings of the lesser frames. The public had been sold on the idea of twins; if they wanted a Norton twin it had to be in a Featherbed frame. And Norton could not supply them quickly enough.

Change Partners

However, another factor was about to play a more influential role in Norton's future. In 1952, Charles Anthony Vandervell, Norton's chairman, was eighty-one years old; his business interests were considerable and the problem of death duties concerned him. In putting his financial affairs in order it was decided that

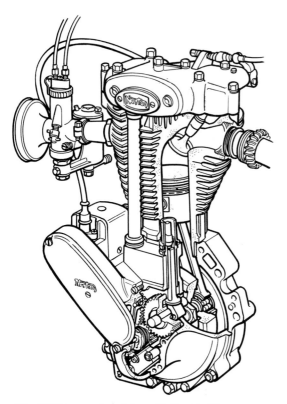

The OHV as produced from 1948–56. The sliding tappets and one-piece rocker box were new for 1948. The head and barrel were still made of cast iron during this time but an alloy head was introduced in 1956 (although the 500T had been fitted with both head and barrel in alloy). The same basic engine was fitted to both the ES2 and the Model 18. The Models 50 and 19 used smaller or bigger versions of the same design.

Norton Motors Ltd and R.T. Shelley Ltd, now Nortons subsidiary company, should be floated on the Stock Exchange. An anonymous bidder made an offer for a majority shareholding and it was accepted. On 24 February 1953 Associated Motor Cycles (AMC) announced that they were to be the new owners. AMC were manufacturers of AJS and Matchless motorcycles and also the James and Francis Barnett lightweights. It was intended that the two companies would be run separately and that Gilbert Smith would stay on in charge of Norton. There would, of course, be a degree of co-operation between the two factories for their mutual benefit. The staff at Norton could not help but feel uneasy: any improvement in the company's efficiency would be bound to involve some changes, and not necessarily pleasant ones. It should be said, though, that there were ways in which Norton could benefit from the takeover, not least from the sales and distribution organization that AMC controlled. AMC were enjoying the best years they had ever had and their sales and profitability were enviable. A sum in the region of £1,000,000 was paid for Norton Motors and R.T. Shelley. After forty years with the Vandervell family, Norton Motors had passed into the hands of their rivals.

A Farewell to Old Friends

Any change in Norton policy was not apparent in the range for 1954 but a rationalization plan had begun. Two new models appeared, or rather two new versions of an old model: the 19R and the 19S. These were 600cc singles with either a rigid frame (19R) or a swinging-arm frame (19S). As their engine dimensions were the same as those of the Big Four and they shared many components no great expense was required to produce them. (Along with the other models in the range they had a new circular plastic tank badge, a departure for Norton but similar to that found on AMC's established products.) It is likely that the sole purpose of the 19R was to help use up Norton's stock of rigid frames. Within a year, all the machines that used the rigid frame disappeared from the Norton catalogue. Out went the Big Four – the bike which had begun life as James Norton's Model 1, the first real Norton. With it went its smaller brother the 16H, the short-lived 19R, the 500T and the Model 18. ('New' 16Hs continued to be available for some years after: as late as 1958 Pride and Clarke were offering unregistered ex-WD models at the bargain price of £39 10s.)

The 19S survived until 1958 although it had little appeal in a market dominated by ever more powerful twin-cylinder machines. The 19S weighed nearly 400lb (181kg) and produced 25bhp. It was not particularly cheap either: around £230 in 1955. At the same time, Panther were selling their 600cc single for £208 and Triumph and BSA were producing 650cc twins which cost only five pounds more than the Norton single. Still, there were those – sidecar enthusiasts mostly – who preferred big singles and the 19S filled a niche. (Sidecars were still a common feature in the 1950s; over sixty different models were available.) A more illustrious model was also dropped in 1958: the Inter. The Model 30 and Model 40 Internationals had been produced to special order only since 1956. However, the appeal of the twin had increased as its performance increased and the Inter was no longer the fastest thing on the road. In 1957 it cost more than the latest model Dominator and was less 'civilized'. The Inter was expensive to produce, difficult to service (relative to the twins) and lacked the 'star quality' it had

once had. AMC had no reason to be nostalgic about it, and so it too was dropped from the range.

Singular Improvements

Towards the end of 1955 an old model reappeared: the Model 50. It was really only a 350cc version of the ES2 (which itself might be considered a smaller version of the 600cc 19S). The ES2 was not the most exciting motorcycle of that period: 25bhp, 380lb (173kg) and with the standard frame. The Model 50 was further handicapped by having 20 per cent less power to haul around just as much weight. In 1956 the Model 50, the ES2 and the 19S received the variation of the Norton gearbox known as the AMC 'box. Little different from the Norton item and no better, the new gearbox was cheaper to produce and was fitted as standard throughout the AMC heavyweight range. The following year all three models were fitted with a new cylinder head which, for the first time on an overhead valve Norton, incorporated a carburettor flange. Most manufacturers had long since adopted flanged carburettors but Norton were different. (When Amal stopped production of stub-fitting carburettors Norton had produced an adaptor and carried on using their old-style cylinder head.) Now progress caught up with them. The new head also featured integral push-rod tubes and increased finning, making it similar in appearance to AMC's other singles: a move towards a 'corporate identity' which, perhaps, was not necessary.

Various minor modifications were made to the singles in the late 1950s. Something more radical was announced in September 1958: the ES2 and Model 50 were to receive the definite benefit of the Featherbed frame.

Although hampered by their lowly power output, the singles now had the best frame available. Overweight and underpowered though it was, the Model 50 could now maintain its top speed of 70mph (112kph) not just up hill (possibly) or down dale (certainly) but also round corners. The Featherbed frame and the cycle parts that came with it gave the ES2 and Model 50 an appeal that they had not had for years. Although it did not make them best-sellers it made them better motorcycles. It also made them ideal 'donor vehicles' in later years when the Triton and other Featherbed-framed specials became popular. In 1958 the ES2 cost £242 and the Model 50 £236 (about £40 less than the Dominator).

The Twins Take Over

The Model 7 had proved to be a best-seller and Norton could not make enough to satisfy demand. There was little wrong with it, even in its earliest form, and only very minor alterations were made in the first few years of production. The front brake was improved (in 1951 and again in 1954) and the cast-iron cylinder head replaced by an alloy head in 1954. Its popularity faded only with the introduction of superior variants. It was eventually dropped from the range in 1956. The appearance and subsequent success of the Featherbed frame emphasized the shortcomings of the Model 7's plunger frame. It was only natural that the twin engine should be tried out in the Featherbed frame (not for racing purposes, of course) and a number of prototypes were seen in 1951.

Visitors to the Earls Court Motorcycle Show in November 1951 got their first glimpse of the new, Featherbed-framed 'Dominator De-Luxe', the Model 88. They were unable, however, to put in an order for

one: once again it was 'Export Only'. It would be available to the British public, but no one could say when, although a price for the home market was given: £204 plus £56 13s. 4d. Purchase Tax. It was 1953 before the 88 went on sale in Britain.

The Model 88 weighed 380lb (173kg), over 30lb (14kg) less than the Model 7, a worthwhile reduction. Its biggest advantage, though, was its superior handling. Norton's twin had been in demand before, but in the new Featherbed frame it was even more desirable. The Model 88 used a version of the Featherbed frame with a bolted-up sub-frame. This arrangement had proved unsatisfactory on the works' racers and so it was with the road bikes. From 1956 on they too used a welded-up sub-frame. Peculiarly, the 88 had originally had its mudguard mounted on the fork shrouds, making it look a little ungainly. This was replaced in 1953 with a smaller mudguard mounted on the lower fork legs.

It must be LOV. Announced in November 1951 the Featherbed-framed Dominator De-Luxe was not available in Britain until 1953. The couple in the picture think it was worth waiting for.

The Model 88 received the minor improvements visited on the Model 7 during the next few years. Late in 1955 it was joined by another model, the 99. This was similar in appearance to the 88 but had a 600cc engine. The extra capacity was obtained by increasing the bore from 66mm to 68mm and the stroke from 72.6mm to 82mm. A slightly larger carburettor and sportier camshaft helped to provide a little extra power. Ariel, BSA, Triumph and Royal Enfield had all been producing larger capacity twins for some time and Norton had to follow suit. Full-width alloy hubs appeared on both wheels – 8-inch front, 7-inch rear – providing the style which was to remain with the 'Dommy' to the end of its production run. The 99 appeared in November at the Motorcycle Show alongside the new Model 50, a bike which was described by *Motor Cycling* as 'a welcome return to the ranks of fast-moving 350s'.

Keeping to their traditional practice of 'mixing and matching', Norton put the 99 engine in a 'standard' frame in 1956 to create the 77. This was a replacement for the Model 7, which was dropped the same year. Norton considered the Featherbed frame unsuitable for sidecar work (although it was used in sidecar racing). The 77 was created for this role and the frame incorporated sidecar fitting lugs as standard. The 77 was a short-lived model, being dropped from the range late in 1958. Another means of using up old stock frames, perhaps? Sidecars were fitted to Featherbed frames in later years with no more adverse effect upon the frame's integrity than might normally be expected.

The separate magneto and dynamo fitted to Norton twins were phased out over the next few years as Lucas concentrated on producing alternators and coil ignition systems. A mixture of alternator and magneto was used on the Nomad, produced in 1958. This was an off-road bike built for America, to compete in enduros and desert races. It was basically a 77 with a 'hop up' kit: higher compression pistons, twin carburettors, two-into-one exhaust and typical enduro styling. It was more powerful than the 77, with a claimed 36bhp at 6,000rpm. It weighed 400lb (182kg); riding it hard across rough terrain must have been interesting.

The Jubilee

Less interesting to ride was the 250cc twin that was introduced in 1958, the Jubilee. The decision to enter the lightweight market had been made two years earlier. Bert Hopwood had returned to Norton as Executive Director in charge of production and product design and the job of producing a suitable machine was given to him. He had been appointed by AMC's Managing Director, without reference to Gilbert Smith, a situation which initially annoyed the Norton MD. Fortunately, Hopwood and Smith both had Norton's interests at heart and they also became united in their dislike of AMC's attitudes towards the company. Although employed by AMC, Hopwood received little assistance from them. His first design for a 250 had been rejected by AMC and the Jubilee (considered by Hopwood himself to be an inferior design) was its replacement. The launch of the new bike coincided with the company's sixtieth anniversary, their Diamond Jubilee. Naturally the new model was called the Jubilee. At the 1958 Show, a gold-plated Jubilee was displayed, the factory choosing to celebrate the Golden Jubilee (fifty years since the first real Norton): cheaper, obviously, to gold-plate the new bike than to encrust it with diamonds.

The new model was not a success. Despite what was described as some of the most

The Jubilee

The Norton Jubilee appeared in response to the demand for lightweight motorcycles which sprang up in the mid-1950s. AMC already produced a number of small two-stroke models but the Jubilee was intended to be a match for the more sophisticated European bikes.

The engine was a unit construction parallel twin, with oversquare dimensions of 60×44mm giving it a capacity of 249cc. The one-piece flywheel assembly had a narrow central flywheel with short alloy con-rods. The right-side crankshaft drove the oil pump and, via an intermediate gear, the two camshafts. The cams were placed high in the crankcases and the cam followers were housed in the iron barrels. (Separate cylinder barrels were used for the left- and right-hand bores, although the 350cc and 400cc versions used a one-piece casting.) Short alloy pushrods operated the rockers which had eccentric shafts to provide valve clearance. Four separate covers enclosed the valves. The cylinder heads were separate alloy castings with wide-angled exhaust ports. The inlet tracts were parallel but a Y-shaped mounting was fitted to accommodate a single Amal carburettor. The left-side engine shaft carried the alternator and transmitted drive to the clutch via a duplex primary chain. A four-speed gearbox was used based on the established AMC gearbox, with kickstart and change lever on the right side.

The Jubilee was launched in 1958. Early production models suffered from crankshaft failures which gave the bike an undesirable reputation. There were other problems too and the engine was noisy and vibratory. The styling was dubious and the quality of the cycle parts was poor. The 350cc version, the Navigator, introduced in 1960 was only slightly better. The lightweight twins were a failure. They faded away in the early 1960s and died during the AMC crash in 1966.

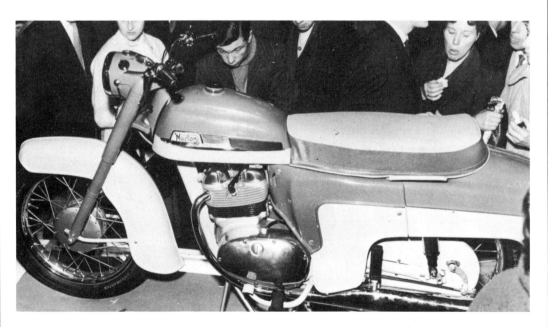

Mixed reaction for the new Norton Jubilee at the 1958 Show. All things considered, the girl on the right, with the dark coat, just about sums it up.

rigorous testing ever given to a motorcycle there were problems with the production models. Early examples suffered crankshaft failures which gave the bike a bad name it never really recovered from. This apart, the engine was noisy and vibrated badly, particularly when it was revved hard. And it had to be revved hard to get to its top speed of 75mph (120kph). British motorcyclists were not used to taking an engine to 7,750rpm, at which speeds the engine felt distinctly uncomfortable. There were also problems with oil leaks, the cam followers and the Wipac ignition system. The public might have put up with these if the bike had not been so gutless: 16bhp pulling 350lb (159kg) around did not give a sparkling performance. Added to this were cycle parts from the Francis Barnett range which were neither attractive nor efficient (the front forks and brakes were used to dealing with much lighter Francis Barnett models). Finally, the price was unacceptable: the Jubilee cost £215 in 1958. A 350cc Royal Enfield cost less and rival 250s from Francis Barnett and BSA cost £185 and £165 respectively. The 200cc Triumph Tiger Cub cost £150. The lightweight market at that time was a competitive place. Apart from a host of British manufacturers there were over twenty-five foreign factories producing two-wheelers in the under-250cc class. Even the advent of a 250cc limit for learners in 1960 could not save the Jubilee from flopping.

Win Some, Lose Some

The 1950s were a decade of very mixed fortunes as far as Norton's racing efforts were concerned. The Featherbed frame had returned the cammy singles to the forefront of international racing, but it could only be a brief respite. Other factories would eventually adapt the technology behind the new frame and then Norton's advantage would be gone. At the start of the decade there were bikes with two-, three- and four-cylinder engines which were more powerful than Norton's single. They lacked its reliability and handling, but both of these problems could be overcome. The 1950 World Championship was an indicator of the situation: Umberto Masetti on a four-cylinder Gilera took the title; runner up, and only one point behind, was Norton rider Geoff Duke.

The works' bikes for the 1951 season showed evidence of Joe Craig's usual steady development. Shorter strokes and larger bores were introduced in the quest for higher revs and Amal's new GP carburettor with its remote float bowl was fitted. The rear sub-frame was now welded to the main frame and the rear suspension units were improved. It was enough to enable Geoff Duke to win the Junior and the Senior TT that year and the first ever 350/500cc double world championship.

Works' riders Duke and Reg Armstrong were first and second in the Junior TT the following year but things did not go so smoothly in the Senior. The chief threat was Les Graham on the new MV four, its engine designed by Piero Remor, who had been partly responsible for the successful Gilera four. Duke led the race at first, but was forced out with clutch problems. Les Graham, on the MV, gave Armstrong a hard time but an oil leak and a long pit stop put him behind the Norton rider at the finish. Only just though, for Armstrong's primary chain broke when he crossed the finishing line – Graham nearly won MV's first Senior TT. (A few days earlier, Cecil Sandford had won the Lightweight TT for MV.)

Increased finning on the barrel and a larger, alloy camshaft drive-tube were external clues

Geoff Duke en route *to winning the Senior TT in 1951, a repeat of his previous year's performance and part of a personal TT double. Duke, a recruit from the factory's trials team, won four consecutive TTs for Norton. He moved to Gilera in 1953 when Norton withdrew from the world championship series.*

to the off-season development of the works' bikes that year. Internally, the stroke had been reduced even further, to near-square dimensions: 85.93×86mm. The engine benefited from the attention of Norton's Leo Kusmicki, who also improved the port shapes and the cam design. (These benefits were passed on to Tony Vandervell and used in his Vanwall engine. Kusmicki was a Polish *émigré* and a talented engineer but was undervalued at Norton despite his abilities. He later went to work for Vandervell and contributed to the success of the Vanwall.)

The Manx engine at this time was producing just over 44bhp at 7,000 rpm, but it wasn't enough: the MV was producing 50bhp and the Gilera over 60bhp. The Nortons had the advantage at circuits where handling mattered most but the Italians were coming to terms with frame technology. That year Norton won seven out of the eight major races in the 350cc class, Duke taking the World Championship once again. The senior class was a different matter; the 500cc Championship went back to Gilera's Masetti, with Les Graham and MV Agusta second.

Duke Departs, Amm Arrives

Norton's financial position worsened during 1952. Development of the four-cylinder engine had been floundering for some time, so it was only natural that the project was dropped. The cancellation of the four was a deciding factor in the departure of works' riders Duke and Armstrong. They both moved to Gilera; the Italian factory meant business that year, fielding as many as six works' bikes at a time. Not surprisingly Duke took the 500cc World Championship in 1953.

Norton may have given up on the four but they carried on racing. The 500cc engine went 'oversquare' (88×82mm) to permit higher revs and oil-cooled exhaust valves were introduced with an external oil-cooling 'gill' plumbed into the lubrication system. More unusual was an experimental low-lying 350 that was seen on a number of occasions. This was based on the Featherbed frame but modified to allow the rider to adopt a kneeling position, draped around the engine. The petrol tank was replaced by 'pods' on each side of the engine, in line with the wheel spindles. These doubled as supports for the rider's legs. A 'dustbin'-type fairing enclosed the front of the bike and another fairing covered the rear wheel. Previously, Norton had ignored aerodynamic aids, but the continental factories had proved their worth (Guzzi, particularly, as they had their own wind tunnel). The device was known variously as 'The Flying Fish', 'The Silver Fish' and, when ridden by new team member Ray Amm, 'The Amm Sandwich'.

The kneeler was raced once, at the North West 200cc, but engine troubles forced its retirement. It was also tried in practice at the TT but not actually raced – it is said that the scrutineer refused to pass it. A leading-link front fork was also seen but again, only in

Flying Fish. Ray Amm lands the Silver Fish uncomfortably at Ballagaraghyn in practice for the 1953 TT. The kneeler was another of Rex McCandless's unconventional designs. FIM regulations curtailed the bike's competition life but internal politics at Norton didn't give it much encouragement either – even though it was used to net the factory over sixty world records.

practice. Instead, Amm and team mates Ken Kavanagh and Jack Brett rode conventional Manxes. (The Amm Sandwich did re-appear later in the year. Norton used it in 350 and 500 form to take sixty-one world records at Monthlery. Its top speed, in 500 form, was 145mph (232kph).

Conventional or not, the works' bikes were good enough to give the factory victory in the 350cc race. Amm and Kavanagh finished first and second, with Jack Brett fourth. The fly in the ointment, so to speak, was Fergus Anderson on a 320cc Moto Guzzi. This was powered by a single-cylinder engine too: a stretched version of Guzzi's four-valve 250. The idea to increase the engine size had originally come from Joe Craig, of all people! He had seen the 250 in practice earlier in the year and jokingly suggested that Moto Guzzi turn it into a 350, which they did. The idea took root and Guzzi went on to produce a proper 350cc engine with which they dominated the class for the next five years. It was a very different 350 from Norton's. Being a scaled-up 250 rather than a scaled-down 500, it weighed only 220lb (100kg) when Norton's 350 weighed 290lb (132kg). It also had the benefit of highly efficient streamlining, developed in Moto Guzzi's own wind tunnel.

Hard Pressed

Prospects for the Senior TT in 1953 did not look so rosy. Duke and Armstrong were making their first appearances on the Gilera four and Les Graham was there with the MV Agusta. Duke's ability, his knowledge of the course (he held the lap record) and the power of the Gilera (an alleged 65bhp to the Norton's 46) made him the favourite. No one was surprised when Duke broke the lap record on the first lap and pulled out a 38-second lead over Les Graham; Amm and Kavanagh taking the next two places. On the second lap Graham lost control of the MV at the bottom of Bray Hill and was killed instantly. The race continued. Duke broke the record again on his second lap but Amm, riding recklessly as he so often did, somehow managed to take the

lead on the next lap. Duke's third lap produced another record time, but Amm bettered it (by three seconds). Duke was aware of the pressure and, trying too hard on a bike that he was not totally familiar with, came off on the exit from Quarter Bridge: Amm was in the clear. Unfortunately he too crashed, on the seventh lap. It was not too serious, though, and Amm was soon back in the race minus a footrest. This let Armstrong on the second Gilera in with a chance. Or it would have, if his chain had not jumped a sprocket. The time he took to replace it dropped him to third place and Amm and Kavanagh finished first and second.

Joe Craig followed a familiar route with works' motors for 1954: even shorter strokes. So short, in fact, (78×73mm for the 350 and 90×78.4mm for the 500) that it was necessary to put the flywheel outside the engine in order to provide enough clearance between the piston and the crank. A five-speed gearbox was fitted for the first time, to cope with the narrow power band of the '90 bore' engine (as it became known). The record-breaking session at Monthlery the year before had shown Craig the importance of streamlining. The new works' bikes were fitted with fairings which were hideous in appearance but helped to improve performance. The long snout of the upper part of the fairing brought the bikes their 'Proboscis' nickname. The lower half of the fairing contained extra petrol tanks which would allow the bike to complete the TT without stopping for fuel.

Ray Amm started the Senior TT with 11 gallons (50 litres) of fuel, the weight of which affected both the handling and the performance of the Norton. As the race proceeded, the load was reduced, the handling and performance improved and so did Amm's lap times. Bad weather had delayed the start of the race and also kept the lap speeds down.

The conditions affected the Gileras more, with their excessive power, but on the fourth lap it appeared that the weather was beginning to improve. Duke had made his fuel stop at the end of his third lap and was ready to go after Amm. Rightly or wrongly the decision was made (owing to the weather) to stop the race at the end of the fourth lap, when Amm was over a minute in front. It was a controversial decision, but it was upheld and Norton won their eighteenth Senior TT.

Ray Amm taking the 'Prosboscis' Norton to its controversial win in the 1954 Senior TT. The lower portions of the fairing contained additional petrol tanks which would have enabled Amm to complete the race without stopping to take on fuel. Any time this saved may have been offset by the adverse effect of carrying 11 gallons (50 litres) of petrol.

A Change in Policy

Before the 1955 season kicked off, Gilbert Smith, Norton's Managing Director, made an announcement regarding racing policy: Norton Motors Ltd would not be entering a works' team in the World Championship series, with the exception of the Isle of Man TT. It was stated that streamlining for non-factory riders was 'undesirable' as it 'added greatly to the first cost of the machine, was costly to maintain' and could be dangerous in certain circumstances. It was felt that works' machines 'would lead to the demise of the private owner'. Norton were to revert to their original policy of racing a type of machine that was available to private owners. Effectively, it meant that the Norton racing development programme was over.

The pronouncement on streamlining was a red herring. Norton could no longer afford to develop the racing single. It was simply outclassed and a replacement multi would be prohibitively expensive. (In fact, Joe Craig had approached a French designer, Jean Nougier, for the rights to his little-known but successful four-cylinder 500; a figure of £3,000 had been agreed for the rights to it, but the deal never came off.) Norton were facing bankruptcy and the parent AMC company did little to help. It was felt that there was no value in racing abroad, particularly as import tariffs often prevented entry into foreign markets (and anyway, Norton were not well placed to take advantage of export markets).

Ray Amm had seen the signs and departed to Italy and MV Agusta but his career never got off the ground; he died following an accident in the first race of the season.

Only minor improvements appeared on the bikes that Norton fielded in 1955, ridden by John Surtees, John Hartle and Jack Brett. It was only years later that the real 1955 works' Norton was revealed: a 'flat' single, similar to the Moto Guzzi. Its success, particularly in the Senior class, would have been unlikely but not impossible; however, it never happened. The project was shelved and development concentrated on conventional machines. Some years later Doug Hele did tests on the cylinder head for the flat engine and found that the exhaust-pipe layout would have restricted the power output to less than that of the standard engine. (During the early 1950s Norton considered a number of unconventional features for their racers. One of these was a rotary valve cylinder head, the work of the decidedly unconventional Laurie Bond. Bond worked at Norton developing this cylinder head but, as with many of his projects, it was flawed and doomed to failure.)

The Junior TT was won by the fully-faired 350cc Guzzi single, second place going to a privately entered Norton ridden by Bob McIntyre. It too had a full fairing. Another Guzzi was third and the works' Norton trailed home behind that. The Senior TT went to Duke and the Gilera. At first it was believed that he had cracked the 100mph (160kph) barrier but it was not to be: the official figure

Norton's secret weapon for the 1955 season. The 'F-type' never made it to the track due to Norton's decision to reduce their racing commitment. The bike aped the layout of the successful Moto Guzzi flat single but it was never completed.

Mechanic Charlie Edwards gives John Surtees some advice at the Isle of Man in 1955. He may have been telling him that the bike nearest the camera needed its clutch adjusting. Surtees had no luck that year – he ran out of petrol in the Senior race but he returned to win the event in 1956. Unfortunately for Norton, he was riding an MV Agusta.

was 99.97mph (159.95kph). Second and third went to Armstrong (Gilera) and Kavanagh (Guzzi). In fourth place was the first works' Norton home, ridden by Jack Brett; Hartle and Surtees both ran out of fuel on the last lap. Surtees made up for it during the year, being almost unbeatable on the home circuits. At one Silverstone meeting in October he even beat Duke and the Gilera. His reward was an offer to ride for MV the next year. It was an offer he accepted. In fact Surtees had approached Gilbert Smith first and told him that Norton could win the World Championship in 1956. New circuits had been included in the series which would give the better-handling Nortons an advantage. He set out his

proposals to Smith, who in reply said that he believed Surtees could win the World Championship with a Norton. The arrangement Surtees proposed, however, would result in the factory paying him more than a director of the company received. To Gilbert Smith that was unthinkable: after all, Surtees was 'only a rider'. Surtees went to MV Agusta for 1956, as did the World Championship.

In November 1955, Joe Craig announced his retirement. Although he had been the Engineering Director, in charge of all engineering and technical aspects, his job was over when Norton gave up 'proper' racing. His salary had been linked to the success of the racing team and any new contract would not be so rewarding. Besides, he had never been interested in anything other than the cammy motors and he would not have been happy getting involved with humbler products. The Norton factory had sacrificed

Surtees on the MV Agusta winning the 1956 Senior TT. Although small, the company was owned by a very wealthy Italian family with a passion for motorcycle racing. They were not afraid to spend the time or money needed to develop multi-cylinder engines. The MV's four-cylinder engine produced 65bhp in 1956 – about 20bhp more than the works' Norton.

When the fast men wore flat 'ats. John Hartle warms up the works' Norton at Crystal Palace in 1956. Hartle was a member of the Norton team in the mid-fifties and a contemporary of John Surtees. He followed Surtees to MV in 1957 and later rode for Gilera.

much to maintain the prestige of the racing singles and Joe Craig had enjoyed something like absolute power as head of racing. It was a position he could not maintain and would not find elsewhere. It was intended that his retirement would not be permanent but that he would take a consultative position elsewhere in the industry. Before this could happen, though, he died in a road accident in March 1957.

A Different Kind of Racing

Norton continued racing after Craig's retirement but with nothing like the commitment they had once had. Improvements were introduced, desmodromic valve gear was experimented with, but the magic had gone. Factory-backed Nortons came second and third to Surtees on the MV in the 1956 TT but had less success the following year, the TT's Golden Jubilee. First Norton rider home in the Senior was Alan Trow in sixth place. It had been a hard race. Entries in the Senior TT included the V8 Guzzi (producing around 75bhp), ridden by Dickie Dale, Surtees on the MV and McIntyre on the Gilera. The race went to McIntyre, who put in four laps exceeding 100mph (160kph). Norton honour was upheld by the strong presence of privateer entries: if you did not have a works' multi, it was really the only bike to have. In 1958, for example, fifteen out of twenty-two finishers in the Senior race rode Nortons.

The racing scene changed totally at the end of 1957, for Gilera, Moto Guzzi and Mondial all agreed to pull out of racing – it was just too expensive. The three Italian companies raced sophisticated machinery which had little connection with the fairly basic models they produced and the rewards from racing could not justify the expense (as Norton had realized). This left MV Agusta with no serious opposition and they went on to score a string of, arguably, hollow victories until the arrival of the Japanese. MV were not primarily a motorcycling company; they raced for the greater glory of the wealthy Agusta family. Norton had already withdrawn factory support but continued to test 'development motors' through selected riders and entrants.

Mike Hailwood's position in the 1958 Junior TT (twelfth) gave little indication of his ability. There was no doubt about it in 1961, when he won the Senior TT at an average of 100.60mph (160.96kph), a swan-song for Norton. This is Hailwood in 1957, at Brands Hatch.

Surtees on the MV had easy victories in the Junior and Senior TTs in 1958. In the Junior the next eleven places were filled by Norton riders, one of whom, in twelfth place, was SMB Hailwood. It was a similar story in 1959, with Surtees again doing the double and Nortons providing the supporting acts. Norton were down at the end of 1959 but they were not quite out for the count. (It is worth noting that the manufacturer's team prize for the Lightweight 125 TT in 1959 was won by an obscure foreign company: Honda.)

Family Problems

The AMC take-over in 1953 had brought Norton few, if any, benefits. It may have seemed like a good move but it was mis-timed and ill-considered. AMC had bought Norton just after Australia, a major export market, had introduced import restrictions. ~Trade agreements with other countries which had been preferential to British manufacturers were also being scrapped. Profits fell and sales became inconsistent. AMC could not afford to modernize their plant, improve their export markets and develop their products, and do the same for Norton. AMC's situation deteriorated through the 1950s. Unable to obtain an exclusivity agreement with Villiers for a new two-stroke engine AMC wasted money developing an unsuccessful engine of their own. This was followed by an attempt to set up a subsidiary company to look after AMC sales in America. It was an expensive failure. It is worth noting also that AMC's management changed during the mid-1950s. Charlie Collier, one of the firm's founders, died in 1953, and many people consider that to have been a turning point in AMC's fortunes: the company stopped being run by motorcyclists and started being run by accountants.

During this period some of AMC's directors developed a dislike for Norton and its management. This created friction between them and Gilbert Smith, in whom the feelings were reciprocated. And as if Norton did not have enough problems coping with an unsympathetic parent company, there were more general problems which affected everyone in the motorcycle business in the 1950s. At home, government policy included trying to control the economy by controlling credit. One year Hire Purchase would be readily available, the next it would be restricted: an unstable situation which did nothing for sales of new motorcycles. The sales of cheaper mopeds and scooters (the majority of foreign origin) increased dramatically during the 1950s, as did 'bubble car' sales after the Suez Crisis. British manufacturers either ignored the ultra-lightweight market, or produced models that were inferior, ill-conceived or, at best, half-hearted offerings: attitudes which were later to be regretted.

In 1955, a 'downturn' year in the British economy, Norton suffered from a feature that was beginning to establish itself in the engineering trade in general: a strike. It concerned a number of men who had been made redundant by Norton but who had found similar work elsewhere. It was not fully supported by the workforce but union action over a six-month period helped Norton to record a loss for the financial year 1955–56. Never a wealthy company, this hit them hard. They received no support from AMC, and struggled through by further reducing staff and improving productivity. It was the abilities of Financial Director Alec Skinner that brought the company through the difficulties and back into profitability. This was a remarkable achievement, especially as Norton were not allowed the facility of a bank overdraft during that period.

A Sad Departure

In 1957 Gilbert Smith's contract of employment expired, and AMC did not renew it. He was very much of the old order and resented AMC's interference in Norton business. Although he may not have been a dynamic Managing Director he had always done what he thought was best for the company. But his ideas and AMC's did not coincide: he had to go. Gilbert Smith had been with Norton since 1916 and a director since 1930; Norton was his life. It is not surprising, perhaps, that he died not long after he retired. He was 62.

For a short while after Gilbert Smith's departure, Norton were without a Managing Director. Alec Skinner and Bert Hopwood ran the company jointly, but then Donald Heather appointed Hopwood to the post. With Skinner's financial acumen and a concerted effort from the workforce Hopwood returned the company to profitability. However, while Norton's fortunes were improving the parent company's were not. Norton were forced to subsidize AMC by providing components (made by Shelley's) at prices below cost. When AMC needed a cash transfusion, Norton were the victims of a 'corporate mugging'. Hopwood's dealing with AMC became increasingly bitter, but he was in no position to do anything about it. Alec Skinner thought otherwise and tried to find a company prepared to buy Norton from AMC. He was unsuccessful and his attempts were not viewed with favour by the AMC board when they got to hear about it. (This period is dealt with by Hopwood in his book *Whatever Happened to the British Motorcycle Industry?*. It is an interesting story of his involvement in the industry and the incredible behaviour of the men who were supposed to be in charge. However, this is only one man's version and Hopwood seems to have made a career of moving from one company to another, disagreeing with the majority of people with whom and for whom he worked. But this need not be seen as criticism.)

Norton approached the 1960s having benefited little from the massive expansion of the motorcycle market that had occurred in the past decade. They had improved their sales and profitability slightly but production was still dependent on machinery that was worn out and a factory that owed more to the industrial revolution than the second half of the twentieth century. The involvement with AMC was proving to be more of a leg-iron than a leg-up and the new lightweight twin was a failure. However, there were bright spots: Bert Hopwood had found an effective and enthusiastic American importer (Joe Berliner) and export sales were improving; also, despite AMC involvement, Norton's financial situation was improving, and there were plans to move the company into a newer, more modern factory.

5

Rise and Fall

More Twins

Norton's problems were not apparent to the public at the start of the 1960s. Indeed, things seemed to be going well for the company and they expanded their range. De-Luxe versions of the heavyweight twins became available

When service stations provided service. The enclosed Dominator De Luxe (with slimline Featherbed frame) was introduced in 1960. The upper part of the petrol tank and rear enclosure is light blue, the rest of the paintwork is grey.

alongside the standard models. The De-Luxe models featured bodywork which half-enclosed the rear of the machine and was very similar to the panelling seen on the Jubilee. Perhaps the styling had come about as a result of the scooter boom, for Norton were not the only ones to go in for it. However, it was not wildly successful and the De-Luxe model was dropped from the range in 1963. Both forms of the Dominator received a new version of the Featherbed frame that year. Possibly the only criticism of the frame had been that the width of the seat rails coupled with the height of the seat – 31 inches (79cm) – made standing astride the bike difficult for many riders. To solve this problem a 'slimline' version of the frame was created with a narrowed section at the rear of the petrol tank. The singles carried on using the 'wideline' version for the rest of the year and then followed suit.

The lightweight range was also expanded in 1960. The original Jubilee became known as the De-Luxe model and it was joined by a 'standard' model devoid of the rear enclosure, valanced front mudguard and detachable seat. At £211 it was £7 cheaper than the De-Luxe but had little else to recommend it. Similar in appearance to these two were the pair of 350s that also appeared towards the end of the year. Produced in standard and De-Luxe form, the 350cc Navigator was an improvement on the Jubilee. The new bike had modified steering geometry, a strengthened frame and Norton's famous Roadholder front forks. In addition it was fitted with the front brake from the heavyweight machines. The Navigator's handling and braking were thus much better than the Jubilee's. Better too was the general performance of the 350. The Navigator engine produced 22bhp compared with the 16bhp of the Jubilee, but the Navigator weighed only 5lb more. This gave the 350 a top speed of over 85mph (136kph), about 10mph (16kph) more than the Jubilee. It was not unknown for Jubilees in later years, when spare parts were hard to find, to be fitted with Navigator engines, a modification which appealed to learner riders restricted to 250cc machines. There were few differences between the two engines, the most noticeable difference being that the Navigator engine had a one-piece cylinder barrel and the Jubilee a two-piece barrel.

The Manxman

Of more interest to the Norton enthusiast in 1960 was the arrival of a 650cc twin, the Manxman. This had been produced at the insistence of Joe Berliner, Norton's American distributor. Berliner had taken over American distribution in 1958 and quickly built up a thriving dealer network. He wanted something to match the 650cc twins being produced by Norton's rivals, which were proving popular in America.

The Manxman was developed by Norton's Chief Engineer, Doug Hele. Hele had worked for Norton in the late 1940s before moving to BSA. There he had produced a brilliant 250cc racer, which unfortunately had been stifled by BSA's short-sighted management. He returned to Norton in 1956 at Bert Hopwood's invitation and became Chief Engineer. Hele had been working on a racing version of the 600cc engine over the past few years and

used this experience to produce a powerful but reliable 650. The new bike was produced as an 'Export Only' model at first, but in 1961 it was made available in Britain. The extra capacity of the 650 was produced by lengthening the stroke from 82 to 89mm. The bore remained the same at 68mm to give an actual capacity of 646cc. High-compression pistons, high-performance cams and twin carburettors were fitted along with a new cylinder head design which incorporated down-draught inlet manifolds. To cope with the extra power output the crankshaft was increased in size. Hele had found this to be a weak point on the Dominator when the engine was tuned to any degree. To fit in with the bike's performance image, a rev-counter was included in the specification. High-rise handlebars, chrome mudguards and a garish colour scheme were also thrown in to appeal to American tastes. A more restrained version of the Manxman was released on the home market the following year, where it was more often referred to simply by its engine size.

In 1961 Norton further expanded the Dominator range by introducing 'SS' versions of the 88 and 99. The 'Super Sports' or 'Sports Specials' (both designations were used) were high-performance variants of the 500 and 600, in the manner of the 650. They too were fitted with a high-performance cam, twin carburettors and polished inlet tracts, plus a siamese exhaust system. The performance of both machines was improved accordingly, giving them both top speeds of about 110mph (176kph), although the 99SS had a much better all-round performance. That same year De-Luxe and SS versions of the 650 were released. This gave Norton a nine-strong range of heavyweight twins: three different capacity engines in three different sets of cycle parts. Prices ranged from £284 for the standard 88 to £311 for the 650SS.

Standard model 99 with chrome mudguards (optional extra in 1961). Well restored but slightly non-standard. However, it does have the rear hub-cover, centre stand and the rear frame gusset 'modesty plate' – all of which tended to be discarded by customizers and café-racers.

The Dominator engine had originally been intended as a short-term proposition by its designer, Bert Hopwood. It continued in production into the 1960s for a number of reasons but in the late 1950s Norton had considered its replacement. This was to be a short-stroke 650cc unit construction twin. Unit construction provided a more compact engine and gearbox assembly. It was a feature of many continental machines and one which Norton's rivals were also adopting. Under Bert Hopwood's direction the Unified Twin was developed by Doug Hele and Brian Jones. It was planned that the engine would power a new range of Norton and AMC bikes. It had a simpler cylinder head design than the Dominator which would have made it cheaper to

produce, and it was intended to be more powerful too. A few prototypes were built and tested but the results were not encouraging. Financial problems brought the project to a halt in 1961. Interestingly, Hopwood, Hele and Jones all went to work for the BSA Triumph group shortly afterwards and helped to produce unit construction engines for both marques. Norton carried on with the non-unit Dominator.

A Brief Revival

Doug Hele was still involved with the development of the Manx at the start of the 1960s. The racing budget was much reduced but imagination was not lacking. At the TT in 1960 a 'low-profile' 350cc Manx, known as the 'Lowboy', appeared in practice ridden by Eddie Crooks. The frame was based on the Featherbed but the petrol was carried under the seat and a bicycle-style front fork was used in order to reduce the height of the steering head. The idea was to reduce the overall height of the bike and so reduce wind resistance and lower the centre of gravity. Another 350, with an ultra short stroke engine (86×60mm), outside flywheel and desmodromic valve-gear was tried in practice but neither bike was raced. Both the Junior and the Senior TT were won that year by MV Agustas. Third place in the Senior was taken by Mike Hailwood on a Norton, still the best bike for a privateer to have. Hailwood and Derek Minter both lapped the Island at over 100mph (160kph) on their Nortons, the first singles to do so.

Hailwood had more luck in 1961. He won the Senior TT riding a Norton with an engine which had been specially built for him by legendary tuner Bill Lacey. (Lacey had been involved with the overhead cam engine's design over thirty years earlier.) 'Officially' he had given up preparing engines but was persuaded by Hailwood's father, Stan, to build just one more for Mike to use on the Island. The engine was built up from a collection of production parts with all Lacey's usual meticulous care. It was good enough to allow Hailwood to put in a race average of over 100mph (160kph) – another record attained for Norton. In second place was Bob McIntyre on another Manx (prepared by Joe Potts) and third was taken by yet another Norton. This was the works' Domiracer, ridden by Tom Phillis. The bike was based on the 500 twin engine and had been built by Doug Hele. Norton enthusiasts were more than satisfied at the Isle of Man that year. Earlier in the

week the Junior TT had been won by rising star Phil Read. He had beaten the semi-works MV into second place on his privately entered Manx, and Nortons had also taken third and fourth. Nortons had not won at the TT since the mid-1950s, but the revival was brief and it was not repeated. The glory days had gone for good.

Super Sports

The Dominator range was simplified towards the end of 1962 when the 600cc models were dropped, along with the De Luxe versions of the 500 and the 650. The four remaining models benefited from Doug Hele's experience with the prototype Domiracer. This was based on a production 500 twin engine housed in a modified Manx frame. The whole bike

Derek Minter, the first man to lap the Isle of Man at over 100mph (160kph) on a single cylinder motorcycle. It was 1960 and the bike was a Norton prepared by Steve Lancefield. Minter was an exceptional rider but never obtained a works' contract. He was the undisputed 'King of Brands' in the late fifties and early sixties and is pictured here at the Kent circuit.

weighed only 280lb (127kg), over 30lb (15kg) less than a production Manx. Hele had managed to coax 55bhp out of the engine although it was never developed to its full potential. The solid-skirt pistons, bigger crankshafts and wider flywheels, which were developed on the Domiracer, helped to improve the Dominator. Production racing had become increasingly popular and the Dominator was proving to be a worthwhile machine in both 500 and 650 form.

The 650SS became one of the quintessential machines of the 1960s. Along with the BSA Gold Star and the Triumph Bonneville, the 'Dommy SS' was a favourite machine with enthusiasts of the period. The 'Goldie' had an enviable racing career as a Clubman's machine but it was an intractable road bike, difficult to ride in traffic and needing careful maintenance. The 'Bonnie' had a legendary engine and any number of specialist parts and tuning 'goodies' were available for it, but like most Triumphs it did not handle too well. (It was not until Doug Hele went to work for Triumph that their bikes' handling improved.) Legendary handling was, however, a real feature of the Dominator, courtesy of its Featherbed frame. In 650SS form the Dominator was an ideal production racer and performed well in the long-distance and production races that became popular in the early 1960s. 'Box stock' versions were capable of almost 120mph (190kph) and they had the handling to match. A 650SS in the hands of Phil Read and Brian Setchell won the 1,000km Production Race at Silverstone in 1962 and the Thruxton 500 Mile race, premier events in the production racing calendar.

Endurance

Long-distance road racing became popular in Britain in the 1950s at about the same time that Norton and AMC withdrew from Grand Prix racing. The first Thruxton long-distance event was a nine-hour race for production bikes in 1955. This became the Thruxton 500 Mile race and the pattern for a number of similar events held at Castle Combe, Silverstone, Brands Hatch and Oulton Park. The popularity of these events grew and stars such as Bob McIntyre, Phil Read and Mike Hailwood would compete. Manufacturers saw the importance of these endurance events and soon became involved either directly or through favoured dealers.

One dealer who became involved in endurance racing from the start was Syd Lawton. He had ridden works' Nortons in the early 1950s and entered a Dominator 88 in the first Thruxton event (it came fourth). He had more success with Triumphs and Royal Enfields during this time, but was persuaded to move back to Nortons in the 1960s by Doug Hele. Hele had been involved in development of the 650SS and knew its abilities. Lawton took delivery of the new bike only a fortnight before the Silverstone 1,000 Kilometre race in 1962. It was ridden to victory by Phil Read and Brian Setchell and they repeated their performance in the Thruxton 500 Mile race the following month.

Lawton's meticulous preparation turned the 650SS into a consistent endurance winner – Setchell and Read won the Thruxton 500 in 1964 and Setchell and Derek Woodman won in 1965. Little 'tuning' work was done to the 650SS which was good for 125mph (200kph) in standard form. Syd Lawton used the same 650SS for three years' racing – a tribute to both his and Norton's engineering. It was forced into retirement by a ruling which prevented bikes over three years old from competing.

Bigger Still

At the insistence of Norton's American importer, the Dominator engine was further enlarged, to 745cc. In this form it was known as the Atlas. The 650cc version had sold well in America but it was still considered a 'small' engine in comparison with the homegrown Harleys. The enlarged engine was developed by Doug Hele who insisted that it should be supplied with only a single carburettor and low-compression pistons. This gave the bike a wide power-band but no noticeable increase in top-end power. Unable to appreciate such subtleties, perhaps, the Americans demanded still more performance. The Atlas was soon fitted with twin carburettors and a few were supplied with racing cams, although this last option made the enlarged engine run very

Factory shot of the prototype Atlas destined for the American market (hence the longhorn handlebars). Unable to appreciate subtlety the Americans demanded a still larger version of the Norton twin – they got it with the Atlas.

roughly. Doug Hele's insistence on a low state of tune was based on the knowledge that the Dominator engine could not stand up to being 'stretched' too far. In thirteen years it had grown from 500cc to 750cc and its power output had increased from 29bhp to 49bhp. Such increases were never contemplated in the original design, and it was beginning to show.

Going South

Norton's fortunes looked set to revive in 1962. The Dominator was proving to be successful on the sales floor and the race track, the Domiracer showed promise and the American market was expanding. The AMC group was not doing so well, however, and their problems affected Norton. Norton's profitability had increased at the hands of Bert Hopwood and Alec Skinner but the money was being used to shore up AMC. Norton had built up a cash surplus in 1960 and were on the

Brian Setchell riding the Syd Lawton 650SS to victory at Thruxton in 1963. Apart from a slightly illegal close ratio gearbox (using Manx internals), Lawton's Norton was standard and needed no 'tuning' to turn it into a winner. Meticulous preparation was the key.

113

point of buying modern premises in Birmingham when they were 'mugged' by the AMC directors. It was true that Norton were part of AMC, but it did seem that the financial flow was one-way.

AMC's finances in the late 1950s and early 1960s were shaky. Their share value had fallen from £1 9s. in 1954, the year following their takeover of Norton, to around 5s. in 1961. The takeover had happened at precisely the wrong time for AMC and consequently they had been unable to improve their facilities or update their own range of motorcycles. In the early 1960s the AJS and Matchless range were unexciting and the Francis Barnett and James models were competing against increasingly superior foreign products. Attempts to produce a scooter, to cash in on the lightweight craze following the Suez crisis, and the failed 'in-house' two-stroke engine had done nothing for their reputation or their bank balance. The American subsidiary was a failure that absorbed large amounts of cash but did little else. Such problems could not be ignored forever. In 1961 a group of AMC shareholders tried to bring about a change in the direction of the company but failed. Their action did shake the company up, though.

Bert Hopwood had become increasingly disenchanted with the AMC directors and saw no future for himself or Norton under their control. He left Norton in April 1961, having had an offer from Triumph. His place was taken by Alec Skinner. Skinner did not like what had happened to Norton at AMC's hands and he tried to find a buyer for the company but was unsuccessful. He resigned the following year. Doug Hele also left. He went to join Hopwood at Triumph, where he became responsible for their successful triple in both its road and racing forms. Bert Hopwood's attempt to move Norton to new premises in

1960 had been scuppered by AMC's directors but they did appreciate the need for such a move. The decline in production of AJS and Matchless models had left them with spare capacity at their factory in Plumstead Road, Woolwich, so it was only natural that they should decide to move Norton in. The James factory would accommodate R.T. Shelley and the Bracebridge Street premises could be sold. The plan to move Norton south was announced in July 1962.

The Norton/Shelley 'complex' that had grown up around Bracebridge Street seemed like a relic from the industrial revolution in the early 1960s. A 'dark, satanic mill' encrusted with grime, soaked in oil and full of ancient, worn-out machinery it may have been, but the motorcycles produced there were respected the world over. It was the people who worked at Norton who were important, not the machine tools or the bricks and mortar. Norton had never been a big company; there had probably never been more than 150 people working there at any one time, and they were hard pushed to produce more than 200 bikes a week. The Norton workforce were proud of the company and for most of them it was more than just a job. There were men who had spent most of their lives working for Norton. When AMC transferred Norton's plant to Woolwich they could not take the accumulated experience with it. There were few jobs offered at Woolwich but then there were few Midlanders prepared to move. Only five of Norton's staff went south, and of those only technical adviser John Hudson and draughtsman Dennis Bourne had any real knowledge of Norton's products.

AMC believed that Nortons could be made just as easily in Woolwich as in Birmingham. It wasn't quite the case. Many of the staff at Norton had grown old with their machines and understood their ways. There was often a knack to getting the best from the worn-out plant: the multi-spindle drill that was used on the Dominator crankcase ruined the first 300 pairs it produced. (It seems that although the drill had been shipped safely, its plank had been lost. What plank? The plank that had to be held against the spindle to keep it central!) The engineering drawings that came down from Birmingham were also in a sad state, often tatty and illegible. AMC draughtsman Charles Udall was given the job of resurrecting them and updating them where possible. It was not an easy job and not particularly rewarding (Udall had previously worked for Velocette, where engineering standards of a different order were involved). There were problems, for example, when the clearances of the Dominator main bearings were altered resulting in premature bearing failures. It took nearly two years in all for AMC to sort out Norton production fully. The losses that this incurred plus the cost of moving (over £150,000) must have made AMC's directors wonder whether it had all been worth while.

No More Singles?

The move to AMC's premises in South London spelt the end of the line for the Manx, although production had theoretically stopped in 1961. A number of bikes were released in 1962, having been built up from spares and those produced at AMC in 1963 came from the same source. Even up to the end the factory had carried on updating the Manx. The final models had improved front brakes, larger-capacity oil pumps and a number of minor modifications. Spares production dwindled after the move to Woolwich even though the Manx continued to be the foremost 500cc racer throughout most of the 1960s. The rights to make the Manx, along with any

remaining spares and toolings, were eventually sold to Colin Seeley. Seeley had also bought the rights to AMC's own cammy racers (the 7R and the G50) in which he had a greater interest. The Manx concession was passed on to John Tickle in the late 1960s. He put more energy into producing parts for the Manx engine and even produced a modern version of the bike, using his own frame, which he sold as the Tickle T5.

The overhead cam Norton engine that became known as the Manx has a history unequalled by any other racing engine. It was considered by some to be outdated when it was designed. Certainly no one would have thought when it first raced at the Isle of Man in 1930 that it would still be winning races there, and elsewhere, over thirty years later. That it was, was due to a fortunate combination of circumstances, the likes of which will never be repeated. But it was due also to a combination of personalities, skills and expertise which will never be repeated either. The Manx Norton became the epitome of the racing motorcycle. It made and maintained the reputations of more racing men than any other machine. It also made and maintained the reputation of a small British motorcycle manufacturer better than any amount of advertizing could have done. Its unparalleled track record ensured that the names Manx and Norton would always be 'Unapproachable'.

The move to Woolwich was made during 1963. During that year the last true Norton singles were produced. The ES2 and the Model 50 had changed little following the introduction of the slimline frame in 1961. Mechanically they were little different from their late 1940s predecessors and in specification seemed even older. They had become relics of an earlier era and there was no demand for them. Motorcyclists no longer wanted singles. The large-capacity British twins were in their heyday but even they were beginning to be challenged. In 1963 the Honda CB72 was available for £260 – the same price as the Model 50. The 90mph 250cc twin was the first Japanese bike to be seen in large numbers in Britain. Honda had won ten out of the eleven 250cc Grands Prix in 1961 and taken the first five places in the 250cc TT. The Japanese had arrived.

The ES400

The Japanese had made their mark in America as well. One welcome feature of the Honda lightweights was 'self-starting'. The American importers pressed AMC for this feature to be included on the smaller Norton twins; and perhaps the engine could be increased in size at the same time? In response AMC produced the Electra 400. This was basically a bored-out version of the Navigator fitted with a Lucas starter motor, although it also incorporated a number of improvements including an uprated electrical system and improved gearbox. The rear wheel from the heavy-weight range was fitted, giving the bike excellent braking if nothing else. In an attempt to keep up with the Japanese the Electra was also fitted with indicators – on the ends of the handlebars!

Self-starting was the Electra's *raison d'être*. But what a pity that this very aspect should prove so unreliable. When the engine was cold the starter motor was not always up to its job, although it was adequate when the engine was warm. A commom fault was the failure of the reduction gearing, which would render the starter motor useless. This would not have been so bad if the kickstart mechanism had been utterly reliable but, unfortunately, it was not. The Electra went on sale in

England in July 1963 (as the ES400) and cost £291. It was a good argument for buying Japanese.

Crossbreeds

The standard versions of the 500cc and 650cc twins were dropped for 1964, leaving just the Super Sports models available. They were joined by the 750cc Atlas. This had previously been sold only for export or police use but was made available in Britain for £358, only £7 more than the 650SS. It had twin carburettors, 12-volt electrics and, like the 650SS, magneto ignition.

The Atlas engine began to appear in other AMC models that year. The AMC sales department were keenly aware of the poor sales of the big AJS and Matchless twins and asked for a Norton-engined model. The idea appealed to the accountants too, and so the Matchless G15 and AJS 33 were born. They both used the Norton engine, forks and wheels but everything else came from the AMC parts bin. They were touring bikes but further mutations appeared in the form of the CSR sports models. These had clip-ons, swept-back exhausts and rear-set footrests (rev-counter an optional extra) amongst their specifications.

Further cross-breeding occurred as AMC attempted to improve sales. In late 1964 new versions of the ES2 and Model 50 were introduced – these though showed little Norton influence. They both had Norton badges on their tanks and used Norton wheels and forks but everything else was pure Matchless. The Model 50 MkII was really a G3 and the ES2 MkII was a G80. Both bikes used Matchless engines in their most unattractive coil ignition form and their overall styling was uninspired.

Norton engine, forks and wheels Matchless frame: it's a G15 Mk2 (the Mk1 used the overbored Matchless engine and was a short-lived horror). This is one of the first and differs slightly from production versions. Originally intended to give AMC dealers in America something worth selling, the model (and its AJS counterpart, the 33) went on sale in Britain in 1965.

The End of AMC

By the mid-1960s AMC were slithering down the slope to bankruptcy. The transplanting of Norton and R.T. Shelley had disrupted production and cost a lot of money. The demand for motorcycles was dropping and AMC were ill-equipped to compete in an increasingly fierce market. BSA and Triumph had recently updated their models, producing new unit construction engines and were increasing their share of the market. The Japanese were taking over the lightweight market and beginning to move up the range. AMC's products began to look increasingly dated. Their mix-

and-match policy could not hide a lack of ideas or an inability to produce new models. Rumours about their financial position began to circulate.

The rumours became facts, and in August 1966 a receiver was appointed to take over AMC's affairs. Between 1961 and 1965 AMC had recorded losses of £2.2 million, a heavy sum for a company whose assets were around £3 million. There had been a brief recovery in 1965 but it could not be sustained. The possibility of a financial package from the company's American distributor was discussed but it never happened. Instead, AMC was bought by a British company, Villiers En-

117

gineering – the same company that had supplied engines for AMC's James and Francis Barnett ranges. In fact, not quite the same company, for Villiers had also experienced severe financial difficulties and had been bought from the hands of the receivers by Manganese Bronze Holdings in 1965. MBH had started life as a small, specialist engineering company but had grown into a medium-sized financial concern. Its rise had been brought about chiefly by the man who was its Chairman in 1966, Dennis Poore. Poore possessed many of the attributes which had been lacking in AMC's management in recent years. He was a qualified engineer (with a degree from King's College, Cambridge) but was also an astute businessman and successful financier. He had raced Aston Martins at Le Mans and had won the British Hillclimb Championship. He was ideally suited to revive AMC's fortunes.

AMC's employees were introduced to Dennis Poore at a meeting in the staff canteen. Instead of taking the stage with AMC's directors he stood on a table amongst the staff and explained who Manganese Bronze were and what their plans were for the company. It was a novel approach and in adopting it Poore literally distanced himself from the directors. With the exception of Charles Udall, the board was dismissed.

An announcement was made in the motorcycling press in October stating that a new company, Norton Matchless Ltd, had been formed. The five marques under its wing – Norton, Matchless, AJS, James and Francis Barnett – would be restored 'to their former pre-eminence in world motor cycling spheres', and plans were 'nearing completion for launching a world-wide sales drive.' The statement helped to restore confidence in what had been AMC but as a prophecy it was only half true. Careful analysis of the motorcycle market showed that there was no place for the James and Francis Barnett marques. The lightweight class had been ignored for too long by British manufacturers and their products were no match for the Japanese or even the European companies. The same was true also of the Norton lightweights. Production of the Electra and the Navigator had ceased in 1965, leaving the Jubilee as the sole representative of the type. But even it did not feature in the range announced for 1967 and no one was really sorry to see it go. The same was true of the 'badge engineered' Norton singles, the ES2 and Model 50 MkIIs. Also missing from the 1967 range were the AMC twins. Their sales had been disappointing in recent years and the larger versions were no match for the Norton. They were also expensive to produce and it was often rumoured that AMC lost money on each one they produced. Such a situation is possible. Accurate per item costing was not a widespread practice at the time and motorcycles were often priced by comparison and not by cost. (It was a feature of the car industry too: BMC lost money on every Mini they sold by pricing it 'competitively'.)

The Norton Matchless range for 1967 included six models which used the Norton twin-cylinder engine. The 750cc version powered the Atlas, the Matchless G15/G15CSR and the AJS 33/33CSR. The 650cc version appeared in the Dominator 650SS, the only other remaining Norton model. The seventh bike in the range was the Matchless G85CS scrambler, a bike which was beginning to lose out to lighter and more powerful machines.

The Need for a New Model

Dennis Poore's experience of the motorcycle business was limited but he quickly recog-

Dennis Poore

Roger Dennistoun Poore was born on 9 August 1916 and educated at Eton and King's College, Cambridge. He graduated with an engineering degree and served in the Second World War as an Engineering Officer in the RAF. He worked in engineering after the war but became more involved in finance. He combined this with a successful career as a racing driver, being a member of the Aston Martin team from 1949–55. He also won the British Hillclimb Championship in 1950.

He was largely responsible for turning Manganese Bronze from a small specialist engineering business into a medium-sized financial concern. He became a director of Manganese Bronze Holdings in 1961 and was Chairman from 1963–87. He was a skilled businessman but was criticized sometimes as being naive, particularly in matters of personnel management. It was said of him that he had an intuitive grasp of business matters and could not always see that others did not. When he saw a course of action that was sensible and logical he would take it and expect others to do likewise. Unfortunately, logic and sense have little place in politics, whether at government or trade union level.

He was distressed by the personal attacks and accusations flung at him during the Meriden dispute: a situation not helped by poor communication and the attentions of the sensationalist Press. Those who worked with him at the time believe that he had the interests of the employees and the future of the motorcycle industry at heart. *The Times* said of him 'He was the impotent victim of ministers and civil servants whose views, he later said, "change more often than the wind." ' He regarded the period as a blot upon MBH's record as well as his own and believed that NVT would not have been forced into bankruptcy if the Government had acted honourably. He gave the receivers more assistance than was necessary, to ensure that the company's debts were discharged. He was often misrepresented by the Press as an asset-stripper, a charge which has little foundation. Supporting the remains of the motorcycle business for over ten years until it was ready to go back into production are certainly not the actions of an asset-stripper. He lived just long enough to see Norton Villiers Triumph pass into safe hands but not long enough to see it selling motorcycles to the public once again. He died on 12 February 1987, aged seventy.

Dennis Poore believed that government involvement in Norton was unavoidable in the seventies; he could never have imagined what the consequences would be.

nized the need for new models and the need to begin production as soon as possible. AMC had been developing a new engine designed by Charles Udall but it was still in the experimental stage in 1966. It was decided that development of this engine would be intensified with the aim of producing a completely new bike for the motorcycle show in September 1967. A number of engineers from Villiers would assist. These included Bernard Hooper, John Favill and Peter Inchley, men

The Z26 looking better than it ever did in life. Designed by Charles Udall for AMC in the early sixties, abandoned due to the company's financial problems, revived by Norton Matchless and finally killed in favour of the Commando the Z26 had an unhappy life. And, fortunately, a short one.

with a wealth of experience in motorcycle engineering. In charge of the team was an ex-Rolls Royce engineer Dr Stefan Bauer, who had been one of Dennis Poore's tutors at Cambridge.

The new engine, codenamed the P10, was an 800cc unit construction twin with chain-driven overhead cams. The design team soon discovered that the P10 was less than perfect. It suffered from lack of power, and from vibration and excessive engine noise. The over-complicated valve-gear, the bottom-end and the cam-chain all had to be redesigned, not to mention the inadequate gearbox. The cam-chain layout was unorthodox and made engine assembly difficult; this was not helped by the length of the chain itself: over 3ft (91.44cm), which was highly unusual and a source of endless problems. During the early part of 1967 the engine was reworked. Ex-AMC draughtsman Tony Denniss redesigned the bottom-end, Bernard Hooper redesigned the head and cam-drive and John Favill worked on an improved gearbox. So much was changed that the engine was given a new codename: the Z26. Charles Udall, who had been under increasing pressure since Norton's absorption, did not get on with the new regime and after a period of sick-leave he resigned.

By the middle of 1967 it was obvious that the Z26 was not going to be ready in time for the Show. The company fell back on the Atlas engine. One of AMC's development engineers, Wally Wyatt, had improved the lubrication system of the old Norton engine and found plenty of extra power at little extra cost. Even in standard form it produced more power than the Z26, although it did not have the appeal of a totally new engine. Unfortunately, though, there was still the drawback of excessive engine vibration. Reduced engine vibration had been pin-pointed as an important feature of the Japanese bikes and it had been decided that it must be a feature of the new Norton too. A rubber-mounting system was being tried on the Z26 but it affected the handling and caused alterations in the drive-chain tension. The solution came from Bernard Hooper: turn the engine, gearbox and swinging arm into a separate sub-assembly and mount that in rubber. This would insulate the rider and the rest of the bike from the vibration but still allow decent handling and constant chain tension. A competition was held within Norton Villiers (of which Norton Matchless was the motorcycle division) to find a name for the new system. 'Isolastic' was the winner.

The engine/transmission 'package' was attached to the frame above the swinging arm, at the front of the crankcases and at the top of the cylinder head. The frame was a new design, built by Bob Trigg to Dr Bauer's specification. As it had originally been intended to house the double overhead cam Z26 engine it was taller than was necessary for the Atlas engine. However, it was no great problem and in 1967 it was still intended that the Z26 would eventually go into production. Roadholder forks with two-way hydraulic damping, Norton hubs and a twin-leading-shoe front brake were used. The bike's styling was handled by a London design consultancy, Wolff Olins. Another competition within the company came up with a suitably aggressive name for the new bike: 'Commando' (very nearly 'Combat').

'Out of the Rut'

Prototypes were tested during the summer of 1967 and the bike was presented to the public at the Earls Court Motorcycle Show in September. It certainly drew plenty of attention.

The designers had given the Commando a slightly futuristic styling. *Motorcycle Sport* said it showed 'a serious attempt to break out of the rut that British big parallel twins have got into'. If the Commando's styling had not attracted attention its colour scheme would have: 'a ghostly unrelieved silver' for most of the bike, plenty of chrome plating and a bright orange seat. Prominently positioned on each side of the petrol tank was a bright green hemisphere, about four inches in diameter. This was the idea of one of Wolff Olin's designers but, like the orange seat, did not become a feature of the production bikes.

The Norton Villiers stand was the centre of attraction at the Show that year, although that was not difficult. The 1967 Earls Court Show was the last of its kind and a particularly

Wolff Olin's design treatment for the Commando. 'Ghostly unrelieved silver' and a bright orange seat. The blob on the petrol tank was bright green and represented a mystical African symbol that would draw people's attention to the bike and make them buy one. Well, they were half-right at least. It was dropped but a reminder of the 'green-eyed monster' lived on in Norton Villiers' circular green logo.

The P11 was produced in response to the American importer's demands for a suitable desert racer to take on the Triumph competition. Using the Atlas engine in a Matchless G85CS frame, it was successful but shortlived. It was also rough, vibratory and relatively fragile.

lacklustre affair. British manufacturers were now few in number and had little to be proud of. They were outnumbered by foreign exhibitors who did not see the Show as being too important. Norton Villiers had more than most to display. As well as the new Commando the Norton name appeared on three other models at the Show: the Atlas, the Dominator 650SS and the P11. The P11 had been introduced earlier in the year and was a development of a Norton/Matchless scrambler that the Americans had been demanding for some time. Various manifestations had appeared briefly from time to time in AJS, Matchless and Norton guises (the Norton derivative had been labelled the N15). The P11 was a little lighter and slightly quicker

than the earlier versions. It benefited from an improved specification which included the Matchless G85CS competition frame and cycle parts, but, as a road bike it was considered inadequate and as a trail bike it was handicapped by its weight. However, it was intended for sale in America where it was well received, off-road activity there being somewhat different from that in Britain.

The price Norton Villiers quoted for the Commando on its introduction was £397 but the bike was not immediately available to British buyers: the export market was more important. Norton wanted to establish the Commando in America, where motorcycle sales were buoyant, before BSA Triumph could get their new three-cylinder 750 into production. There were also rumours of more sophisticated 'superbikes' from Japan. Norton Villiers needed to move quickly.

Into Production

The first Commando prototypes had been put together in only four months and there were still some details to be finalized before the bike could go into production. For reasons best known to themselves, the production engineers had chosen not to incorporate the modification which Wally Wyatt had shown would improve the Commando's perform-ance. The first batch of engines had been produced before Dennis Poore intervened to have the modification introduced retrospec-tively. The 56bhp that the engine was now producing was too much for the standard Norton clutch. This was replaced by an all-new diaphragm clutch which was more pow-erful but lighter in operation. It was designed by Laycock Engineering, experts in car trans-mission systems.

When the bike did get into production, in April 1968, it had a more conventional look. The green globes and the orange seat had gone and so had the 'ghostly' silver paint. There had been problems obtaining a uniform silver, owing to the different techniques re-quired for different components, and it was also felt that it might cause some 'sales resist-ance'. A greater source of sales resistance arose from a fault in the design of the Com-mando's frame: a batch of about 100 bikes were despatched to America but it was dis-covered that the front down-tubes would break within the first few thousand miles. Dr Bauer's team tried a number of modifica-tions but the breakages still occurred. Ken Sprayson of Reynolds Tubes, who made the frames was eventually called in. He came up

The 650SS in 1968 – humpy back seat, twin concentric carburettors and cherry red petrol tank. Spoilt by the high bars but then it is an export model. Time was running out for the Featherbed-framed Norton in 1968 following the arrival of the Commando.

with a solution which was both simple and effective. He added a small tube from the base of the steering head to the main spine tube. Testing was conducted over an Army tank-testing range, the best 'unadorned' frame (with extremely heavy-gauge tubing and com-prehensive gussetting) managing twenty-three circuits of the course before breaking; the Sprayson-modified frame was tested for 280 circuits without breaking. The modifica-tion was incorporated into the design. (The need for such a modification rankled with Dr Bauer. His calculations had shown that the frame was perfect and he did not like to be

Motorcycle News' *'Bike of the Year' in 1968 and the men (and woman) who were responsible (Note: P = Plumstead; W = Wolverhampton): 1. Eddie Bruce (draughtsman W); 2. Bob Trigg (section leader W); 3. Mike Anderson (senior draughtsman W); 4. Wally Wyatt (development department manager P); 5. Tony Denniss (chief designer P); 6. Bernard Hooper (chief designer W); 7. Margaret (surname unknown to the author) (Secretary P); 8. Terry Wetherfield (senior draughtsman P); 9. R. Cakebread (draughtsman P); 10. Roger Jordan (draughtsman W); 11. John Favell (section leader transmission W); 12. Peter Attwood (draughtsman P); 13. Leslie Apps (draughtsman P); 14. Eric Goodfellow (development department fitter P); 15. Trevor Denman (draughtsman P); 16. Bert Lambert (development department fitter P); 17. John McLaren (development engineer P); 18. Charlie Matthews (drawing office clerk P); 19. Bill Booker (development tester P); 20. Anonymous (development tester P).*

proved wrong.) Fortunately, the problem was solved before it could become common knowledge.

Bike of the Year

The Commando was a success: the Press liked it, *Motorcycle News*'s readers liked it (they voted it 'Bike of the Year' from 1968–72) and more importantly the people who bought motorcycles liked it. It cost £456 when it was released in Britain in 1968, considerably more than its Show price but that did not affect sales. It was modern, stylish and it did not vibrate (well, it did really, but you couldn't feel it). It weighed just under 400lb (181kg) which was about 35lb (16kg) less than the Atlas and this was not a bad figure for a big twin. It had a top speed of 115mph (184kph), would do 0–60mph (100kph) in less than seven seconds and it handled well. The Commando ushered in the era of the 'superbike'. It was the first of the breed – but only just. BSA Triumph announced their long-awaited 750cc triple in 1968 and put it on sale in Britain the following year. (It was expensive: £614, over £100 more than the Commando at the time). Yamaha produced their new XS1 650cc overhead cam twin in 1969; Kawasaki released a scorching three-cylinder 500cc two-stroke the same year; and, if that were not enough, Honda came up with an outrageous four-cylinder overhead cam 750.

The Commando sold well from the day it was released. Even when other superbikes came on to the market it remained popular. Its success was due to a combination of many factors. It had a blend of old and new features which enabled it to appeal to a wide range of buyers. The engine and gearbox were a known quantity and not too complex for the average owner or mechanic. Its performance was exciting even if initially it was a little slower than the Triumph or Honda. Its styling was modern but not 'way out'. The new BSAs and Triumphs by comparison were awkward and the Honda four had a curiously clumsy, almost old-fashioned look. These attributes apart, the Norton Commando sold well because it was 'marketed' efficiently. Its image, advertizing and distribution were as carefully considered as its production, if not more so.

Selling the Commando

Dennis Poore was not content just to oversee the development of the new model; he wanted to ensure its success. He did this by looking closely at all aspects of the Commando's distribution and sales. During the winter of 1968–69 Poore went on a whistle-stop tour of America. He analysed Harley-Davidson's dealership network, sales and distribution methods. He also looked at General Motors' sales and distribution methods. He came back convinced that Norton Villiers had to have their own distribution network, not just in America but world-wide. This would give them closer control over distribution and supply, and make planned production easier. It would also give them an extra profit share from each stage of the distribution process. Subsidiary companies were set up to handle distribution at various levels and in various countries. It was an indication of Poore's acumen that he could make this system work whereas AMC had failed miserably with it in America. American sales were divided between Norton's established distributor, Joe Berliner, and a new subsidiary, the Norton Villiers Corporation. Berliner covered the east coast and NVC the west. Poore appointed Bill Colquhoun to look after the American operation. Colquhoun did an excellent job of building up Norton's sales with 'just three men and a tin shed'. Before NVC took over distribution 'west of the Mississippi' Norton sales amounted to about 350 bikes a year. In less than three years Colquhoun had boosted sales to 7,500 a year.

Dennis Poore did not just organize an efficient distribution network in America; he also organized an effective advertising campaign. It was as simple as it was effective. America was the major market for the Commando. The two chief motorcycle magazines in America were *Cycle* and *Cycle World*. Poore booked the inside front cover of them both, every month for five years. No other advertizing was placed. He also organized the actual advertizing content, which was changed every few months and chose the model who appeared with the Commando in its various guises. The model, Viv Neves, became known to motorcyclists as 'The Commando Girl'. At a time when most of the motor and motorcycle industry used mildly pornographic advertising the Commando adverts were restrained and stylish in comparison, and probably more effective for it. The adverts gave the impression that Norton spent a fortune on them but, by block book-

Frank Gillespie storms past Mike Jackson's apposite slogan at Ascot Park, California in 1972. Dirt track success at Ascot did much for Norton sales on the West Coast as did shrewd marketing from NVT's own distribution company.

ing, Poore spent relatively little. The majority of motorcycle enthusiasts saw them, talked about them and never noticed that Norton were not advertising elsewhere.

Any Model You Want, as Long as It's a Commando

The Commando's success spelt the end of the road for the other bikes in the Norton range (and the Z26 project). Production of the Atlas and the P11 (known in its later stages as the P11A and then the Ranger) was phased out in 1968. The same year, the Dominator 650SS was detuned, restyled and renamed. It became the Mercury and last appeared in the Norton lists in 1970, price £390. It was also the last appearance of the Featherbed frame. Twenty years after its introduction the Featherbed frame was still highly regarded and still superior to the frames found on many sophisticated superbikes. For many years it continued to be the first choice for people who built hybrid motorcycles and housed nearly every kind of engine imaginable from Vincent twins to Saab two-strokes to Honda fours.

Motorcycle production was much simplified by concentrating on one basic model. It brought economies of scale and made life easier for parts stockists. Norton Villiers introduced a little variety by producing the 'S-type' Commando in 1969 (and a Police-issue model called the 'Interpol'). The original model became known as the Fastback and continued in production. The S-type had a sportier look, mildly suggestive of a scrambler but nothing like the P11. It had a smaller petrol tank, higher handlebars and a high-level exhaust system which ran along the left side of the bike. There were a number of other minor differences too and some improvements were introduced which were common

to both models. The contact breakers were moved from behind the left side of the timing case to the front of the right side, and enclosed in a circular alloy cover, making them much more accessible. The width of the primary chain case was reduced to improve ground clearance, the rev-counter drive was moved and softer rubber mountings were fitted. Few changes were needed, however, suggesting that Dr Bauer's team had very nearly got it right first time.

The S-type came about following American bike dealers' unfavourable comments about the Fastback. Bill Colquhoun found the Americans were not too keen on the bike's modern styling. He would turn up at a bike shop with a Fastback and try to persuade the dealer to take on a Norton agency. The dealer would turn the offer down, mainly on the grounds that the bike was a little weird. Colquhoun would agree with them and then say that since he was there anyway, why didn't they try a ride on the bike? One quick ride was enough to convert most dealers, and another new agency would open. The Isolastic system was that good, and with the introduction of the S-type sales improved further.

Another Move

In 1969 Norton Villiers announced that they would be moving out of the Plumstead Road premises. The area was scheduled for redevelopment. It was like Bracebridge Street all over again, for many of the people of Plumstead had put in long years at 'Colliers' (the Collier family had founded the Matchless marque and been part of it into the 1950s). And, just as with the move from Bracebridge Street, the company would be moving out of the area. Government policy prevented new industrial development in south London, forc-

The Interpol was Dennis Poore's idea but it was created by Neale Shilton, who was recruited specifically for the job. Despite this, and the steady sales of the model, Shilton was often obstructed by management at various levels who saw the Interpol as a nuisance. An unpleasant reminder of past traffic misdemeanours, perhaps?

ing many companies to move into selected 'growth areas'. There were financial inducements to move to such areas and so Norton Villiers had little choice but to move their motorcycle division to one at Andover, in Hampshire. The old AMC factory carried on making spare parts but was gradually wound down. It closed finally in 1971.

Production of Commandos at East Portway in Andover began in early 1970. In fact the bikes were only assembled there: the massive Villiers factory in Wolverhampton pro-

duced the engines and did most of the machining, and the frames were made by Reynolds in Birmingham. It was intended that the factory at Andover would be increased in size and become self-sufficient. However, problems at Villiers prevented this. Sales of Villiers' industrial engines and generators were falling owing to increased foreign competition, and the management at Villiers were keen to continue producing Commando engines to keep the factory going and retain their jobs. The Villiers factory covered over thirty acres, had excellent facilities, including its own forge and employed over 3,000 people. There was enough spare capacity to absorb Commando engine production. It resulted in a peculiar arrangement whereby parts were shipped down from the Midlands, assembled at Andover and then, in the case of home market bikes, sent back to the Midlands for distribution. It was not a satisfactory arrangement but it carried on for about eighteen months. It ended with Wolverhampton taking over complete production of the Commando, and the Andover premises were given over to storage and distribution of spare parts and despatch of export sales.

More of Same

The Commando range was gradually expanded, although none of the variations were radically different. In 1970 the Roadster was introduced: this was little more than an S-type with a low-level exhaust system and it was no surprise when the S-type was later dropped. The Fastback was updated with higher handlebars, different tank badges, a new exhaust system and other minor changes and became the Fastback MkII. The same year a higher-performance engine, the Combat motor, was offered as an option. Aimed at those who did not think 60bhp was enough, the Combat motor gave 65bhp and soon earned a reputation for being unreliable.

New versions of the Fastback and the Roadster were released the following year – more cosmetic changes – as were three new models. The Hi-Rider was an attempt at a factory 'custom bike'. Choppers and custom bikes were the latest thing in America and Norton Villiers produced one to cash in on the boom. It was little different from the normal

The Roadster, introduced in 1970, was virtually an 'S-type' with low-level pipes. Handlebars apart, it was an attractive machine. The Combat engine which was also introduced in 1970 was less appealing.

Commando but had high bars ('ape-hangers') and a high-backed seat complete with sissy-bar. These were features which identified it as a custom bike but fooled no one. It probably had its admirers in America but in a country where there are people who collect barbed wire nothing is surprising. The ghost of the P11/Ranger reappeared in the form of the Street Scrambler: a dual purpose bike with high-level exhausts, sump-guard, small head-light, etc. This was not a serious attempt at a scrambler but, along with the Hi-Rider, it was an indication that Norton's marketing men had recognized the 'fun market' for motorcycles that had appeared. A little more serious was the third newcomer, the Production Racer. The Commando had been having some success in production racing and the new bike was a ready-to-race model. Combat engine, small fairing, clip-ons, rear-sets, single seat

Oh dear! Well, someone must have liked it. The Hi-Rider stayed in production for four years. An attempt at a customized, factory 'chopper'. Easy Rider had a lot to answer for.

and disc front brakes all helped to improve the racing potential of the bike. Prices for the various models ranged from around £600 for the Fastback to £630 for the Hi-Rider. The Production Racer was considerably more expensive at around £800.

A further Commando variant was introduced in 1972. This was the Interstate. It was similar to the roadster but had a larger petrol tank, indicators, a disc front brake and an even more powerful version of the Combat motor. The Interstate was intended as a high-speed tourer but it was undergeared and many riders would over-rev the engine. The results were inevitable and Norton Villiers received a great many warranty claims. One man who experienced the continual problems caused by the over-stressed Commando engine was Norton Villiers' Service Manager, John Hudson. Hudson had to deal directly with owners and dealers and he realized the size of the problem. His insistence was largely responsible for the improvements that were instituted in 1972 and resulted in a better bike being produced.

Problems

The Commando had needed the Isolastic engine mountings to hide the vibration produced by the 'stretched' Dominator engine. However, it could not hide the other problems that were a result of increasing the capacity and power output far beyond the designer's expectations. The standard Commando engine was producing 60bhp at 6,800rpm in 1970 and bearings in both the engine and the gearbox were unable to take the strain. Great care had to be taken in production and assembly of the engine if it was to be reliable, but the inexperience of the Villiers staff in producing a high-power engine and the need for increased engine production meant that this care was not always taken. Quality control was not what it should have been either, and the Villiers' staff often considered advice from the Service Department and ex-Woolwich designers as unnecessary interference.

The reliability of the standard engine was not helped by American sales brochures which led the Commando owner to believe that it was safe to run the engine at sustained high speeds. This was good advertising copy but bad practice, and it accelerated engine failures. The introduction of the Combat motor, in 1970, did nothing to improve the

situation. It was offered as an option on any bike in the range and was good for around 65bhp. This was achieved by using 'hotter' cams and a higher compression ratio, which put even more strain on the bottom-end (a problem which Doug Hele had foreseen much earlier with the Atlas engine). The compression ratio was increased by machining the cylinder head by 0.5mm but the push-rods were not shortened accordingly. This left the rocker adjustment screws near the end of their adjustment from new, and meant that they were not as secure as they could be. Alterations to the valve guides to accept oil

Planned but never produced. 1973 Interstate with specially designed fairing, panniers and peculiar additional centre stand. Black painted barrel suggests Combat motor, not a desirable option.

seals reduced the support for the valves, and this led to accelerated valve wear and increased oil consumption.

An attempt was made in 1972 to overcome some of the problems, but if anything matters were made worse. Stiffer crankcases were introduced and a more substantial roller bearing replaced the ball race used for the timing-side main bearing. Previously, the crankcases had flexed along with the crankshaft and so damped some of its movement, but the new cases did not permit this. The crankshaft flexing increased and caused the roller bearings to dig into their tracks (which did not happen so much when one side was a ball). Bearing life was thereby considerably re-

Cosworth's Challenge

The engine that Keith Duckworth designed for Norton was more than just 'two cylinders chopped off the Cosworth DFV engine'. It did use DFV technology, particularly in the cylinder-head layout and camshaft form but they accounted for only a small part of the total design. Duckworth spent a great deal of time designing a five-speed 'cassette' gearbox and a system of balance shafts to reduce the engine's inherent vibration. The format of the engine – a 360 degree parallel twin – was one of the parameters specified by Norton which reduced its potential as a racing engine. The need for the same basic engine to be suitable for racing and road use also forced compromises upon the design.

The engine that was to power Norton's new racer – 'The Challenge' – was an upright 747cc twin with a very oversquare bore and stroke of 85.7mm×64.8mm. Twin overhead camshafts were driven by a rubber belt on the left side and worked the valves through inverted bucket tappets. There were two balance shafts: one behind the cylinders driven by the cam-belt and one at the front of the engine driven by gears. Primary transmission was taken from a quill shaft which ran through the front balance shaft to a sprocket on the right side of the engine. A Hy-vo chain carried the drive to the diaphragm clutch. The cross-over gearbox was a five-speed unit with a rotating drum selector. Electronic ignition was used and an alternator on the left end of the front balance shaft provided power for the ignition and the fuel-injection system.

Cosworth produced a number of prototype engines for Norton but the race team never had them running satisfactorily. Fuel injection was abandoned in favour of twin carburettors and even, at one point, a single SU carburettor. Problems with the cooling system and the alternator side-lined the bike on the few occasions it was raced although the main problem was simply lack of development. Norton had been unable to replace Peter Williams as a development engineer and were running into grave financial problems in 1975. The Challenge project fizzled out before it ever really got started.

The world of motorcycle racing is full of 'if only' stories: if only the Challenge engine had been developed, would it have been successful? The answer is yes. In the mid-1980s, one of Cosworth's directors, Bob Graves, took an interest in the Challenge engine. Over the next few years he ironed out the mechanical problems, developed an efficient fuel-injection system and had an unusual but effective 'frame' built for it. It was raced as the Quantel Cosworth (Quantel being another company with which Graves was involved) in the 'Battle of the Twins' series. Raced against more modern twin-cylinder engines specifically built for racing and often with factory backing the Quantel was still a success. With Roger Marshall riding, it won the Daytona event in 1988 against fierce competition from Honda and Ducati. In its final form, the engine produced 120bhp at 10,000rpm, good enough to give the bike a top speed of 178mph (285kph) at Daytona. Bob Graves believed that there was still more power available and that the engine could be lightened considerably, but he had proved his point. The Challenge was a winner. If only Norton had had the time and the money. . . .

duced. Another improvement also backfired: the introduction of an external cartridge-type oil filter. In itself this was a worthwhile item, but it was decided that the gauze filter inside the crankcases was no longer needed. Unfortunately the oil pump came before the oil filter, and any broken pieces of engine had to pass through the pump before they could pass through the filter. In doing so they would wreck the pump. It was an elementary mistake and one which added to the overall problem.

Tony Denniss had foreseen the problem of 'whippy' crankshafts when he had helped to develop the Combat motor at Woolwich. He had specified the use of a particular bearing made by Ransome and Marles. This had a barrel-shaped 'roller' which could accommo-

The SPX Wulf. Two of Norton's design team, Bernard Hooper and John Favill came up with a design for a stepped-piston two-stroke engine and this prototype was produced using Commando cycle parts. It wasn't developed fully before Norton ran into financial problems. Bernard Hooper carried on to develop the engine for light aircraft, military and automotive use.

date the crankshaft whip. The Villiers engineers ignored this specification – a decision they came to regret. In searching for a solution to their self-inflicted problem they came up with the FAG 'Superblend' bearing. This was similar in design (but cheaper) and was almost as effective. The search for reliability also led them to reduce the compression ratio (from 10:1 to 8.5:1) and fit cams with a milder profile. The gearing was raised to prevent the engine being over-revved and give it an easier life at motorway cruising speeds.

The combined improvements introduced during 1972 brought a welcome degree of reliability to the Commando. The modifications were fitted to all the new bikes in stock at Norton Villiers and at their dealers. This affected production considerably and it was not until the following year that things were running smoothly again. In the meantime the company had had to deal with a huge number of warranty claims which had done nothing for

The Challenge engine. Unfairly attacked as being overweight and underpowered the Cosworth-produced twin was almost stillborn. Financial problems and the lack of an effective development team caused the Challenge to be labelled as just another 'British World Beater'.

their reputation or their finances. Both of these features were to come under scrutiny in 1973 and far greater problems were to occupy the company.

Racing Commandos

After the sale of the Domiracer to tuner and specialist parts manufacturer Paul Dunstall in 1962 Norton had not had much involvement as a factory in racing. Private entrants did well with the twins in production racing and long-distance events in the 1960s, and specialist tuners such as Francis Beart, Ray Petty and Steve Lancefield kept the Manx competitive at club and national level. However, it was a foregone conclusion that the Commando would be raced in production events, and Norton Villiers had anticipated this. Co-

operation with Paul Dunstall enabled a series of tuning parts to be available for the Commando as soon as it was released. Paul Smart came second in the 1969 Production TT with a Commando and Peter Williams very nearly won the class the following year. He ran out of fuel in the finishing stages of the race whilst leading, and lost by only 1.6 seconds. Williams had joined the development team at Andover in 1970 but his racing career so far had received no official factory support.

His success in other events and the birth of the Formula 750 class encouraged Williams to persuade Dennis Poore to set up a factory racing team. Williams was eligible for inclusion on two counts: he was a top-class rider and he was a qualified engineer. A team was formed and based at Andover. Williams was joined by two other top British riders, Tony Rutter and Phil Read, and the team was

A thing of beauty and a joy to behold until the main bearings go. The Commando engine, attractive but unreliable. This is a much-improved 1973 version but it's still far from perfect. The cylinder barrel is cast-iron painted to look like alloy.

Not bad for a first attempt. Tony Rutter rides the Mk1 version of the Williams' designed John Player Norton. Top speed of over 150mph (240kph) was possible with a mildly modified Combat engine. Small size and excellent aerodynamics were part of the formula.

managed by an experienced ex-racer, Frank Perris. The team was launched in November 1971 with support from Imperial Tobacco. The John Player Norton racing team was born, and its first objective was the Daytona 200 Mile race to be held the following February.

Williams knew that the Nortons would be the underdogs at Daytona. In racing form the Commando engine produced 70bhp – over 40bhp less than the two-stroke Kawasakis and Suzukis – so he set about making the racing bike as light and as aerodynamically efficient as possible. He spent hours and hours in the wind tunnel refining the bike's fairing, and managed to reduce the bike's overall size to produce a racer that looked more like a 500 than a 750. He also counted on it making fewer refuelling stops than the other bikes. He fitted pannier tanks in between the fairing and the engine to allow the bike to carry over 5 gallons (24 litres) of petrol.

At Daytona the Kawasakis and the Suzukis were timed at over 170mph (270kph). The Norton was slow in comparison at 155mph (250kph), but at least it had superior handling. Phil Read led the race for a while but was beaten back to fourth place, and Williams retired with a broken gearbox – a problem which was to recur throughout the year. The Suzukis and the Kawasakis had their problems too. They broke down during the race and the first three bikes over the line were Yamaha 350s. At the TT Williams managed to take second place in the Production 750 race despite losing fourth gear (the winner was Ray Pickrell on a Triumph Trident). In the Formula 750 race there were more problems for the John Player team. Phil Read retired after one lap with 'engine problems', new recruit John Cooper lost his gear lever (there was no spare!) and Williams was in second place (behind Pickrell again) when his gearbox

packed in. The five-speed gear clusters were provided by transmission specialist Rod Quaife, but even such high quality components could not overcome the problem. After all the gearbox was never designed to cope with 70bhp.

Norton had more luck in the shorter races, which did not put so much strain on the gearbox. Williams won the Hutchinson 100, there was a team success at Scarborough (Mick Grant, Williams and Read) and Read won the Race of the South at Brands Hatch. There were other wins too, including production race successes for Dave Croxford and Mick Grant. It was not the best season imaginable but not bad for a development year.

Williams had more time to prepare for the 1973 season and introduced a number of modifications on the 'MkII' racer. The transmission was improved by the use of a primary chain case which incorporated a third bearing to support the gearbox shaft. This prevented the shaft from flexing, the main cause of the gearbox failures. The engine and gearbox sprocket design was altered, the gearbox 'speeded up' and the gear-profiles changed. It amounted to a major redesign of the transmission system and it worked; there were no more gearbox problems.

Williams did not stop there. He designed a totally new and unorthodox frame for the racer. It was a monocoque construction using a double-skinned mild-steel shell (replaced later in the season by a lighter version in stainless steel). It reduced the centre of gravity and the frontal aspect and improved the weight distribution. It incorporated the petrol and oil tanks but made access to the engine difficult. Again Williams spent hours in the wind tunnel to give the complete bike a low drag coefficient. Williams was such a perfectionist that the riders were not allowed

Peter Williams on his way to winning the 1973 Formula 750 race. The bike used the monocoque chassis that Williams designed but which proved unpopular with the mechanics.

to have lettering stitched on to the backs of their racing leathers in case it disturbed the air flow! New forks were also made for the racer, alloy wheels were fitted and a fabricated swinging arm constructed. The engine received plenty of attention from Williams too. Larger valves, modified valve-gear and steel push-rods were fitted (Williams had discovered that the aluminium push-rods compressed too much to provide accurate valve control). The new racer was slightly heavier than the 1972 version but it was stiffer, lower, leaner and more powerful. Although it still used the standard Atlas engine dimensions of 73×89mm, the MkII racing Commando engine produced 76bhp at 7,500rpm.

Only one example of the monocoque racer was ready in time for Daytona in 1973. There were minor problems with it but at least Peter Williams managed to complete the race. American team mate Dave Aldana rode a 'MkI' version and was forced to retire – with gearbox problems. Back in England Williams had better luck. He won three of the six Transatlantic Trophy races with the MkII John Player Norton against fierce competition from the best American and British riders. He won the F750 race at the Isle of Man and set lap and race records. His best time of 107.27mph (171.63kph) was twenty seconds faster than Ray Pickrell's previous record. The only man who had been round the Island faster was Mike Hailwood (and that was with Grand Prix works' Hondas). Williams also won the Production 750cc race at the TT and a number of other races on the mainland.

Peter Williams and works' Suzuki rider Barry Sheene tied for points that year in the Motor-cycle News Superbike Championship. One of Williams' team mates in 1973, Dave Croxford, was less fortunate. Croxford won the Thruxton 500 Mile race (with Mick Grant) that year and had shown that he had plenty of ability. He did seem to spend an awful lot of time falling off bikes, though (and, it should be said, not just Nortons). He crashed at the Isle of Man, in practice and in the Production race, and he fell off three times in the Hutchinson 100. In his racing career he crashed 189 times but never broke any bones. His most spectacular crash was at Silverstone in 1973 when he dropped the monocoque Norton at Woodcote Corner, doing around 140mph (224kph). The bike was written off. The mechanics in the team eventually forgave him and later pre-sented him with the remains of the bike's monocoque shell, beaten into a coffee table. It was inscribed with the words 'Five weeks to make it. One second to break it.'

The monocoque chassis was a sore point within the team. The mechanics did not like it because it provided little access to the engine for maintenance and was very difficult to repair after a crash. Williams had chosen a monocoque design because he was anticipat-ing delivery of a totally new racing engine in 1974. The designer of the engine was a racing car engineer and more familiar with monoco-que installations. Also, the new engine would be much more powerful and the monocoque would be able to accommodate the extra power. In the meantime Williams was de-veloping the chassis so that it would be fully sorted when the new engine arrived. Never-theless Frank Perris chose to drop the mono-coque at the end of the 1973 season and gave the team mechanics the go-ahead to build a tubular space-frame affair. Perris and Wil-liams did not get on too well together and it is

possible that this decision was an attempt to show who was the boss. Williams was right on this occasion and the 1974 John Player Norton was not as good as its predecessor.

The bike was lighter but it was taller and its weight distribution was not ideal. The petrol tank was too small and extra petrol had to be carried in a tank in the seat hump. This had an adverse effect on the bike's handling. Even with a more powerful, short-stroke engine (77×80mm) the new bike could not match the lap times of the MkII version. There were some wins for the bike at the start of the season but not at the Isle of Man: Williams and Croxford both retired on the first lap of the Formula 750 race. Williams won the Hutch-inson 100 later in the year but two weeks later at Oulton Park disaster struck. The petrol tank came loose causing Williams to fall off the bike while he was cornering at speed. He

The Milan Show 1973. The new John Player Replica, available with the standard 850cc engine or a short stroke 750cc competition unit. A limited edition model, only 300 were produced. (Norton involvement in Italy went beyond just selling bikes there, a number of components for the Commando were also produced in Italy. The quality was not always consistent though, as Norton were to re-learn in the eighties.)

hung on to the handlebars and fought to get back on but could not stop the bike from crashing. It was a horrific accident and Williams was very badly injured.

The accident brought Williams' racing career to an abrupt end. It also removed much of the impetus from the Norton team. They had a few successes during the rest of the season but the Commando-based racers were struggling against the purpose-built Japanese two-strokes and life on the tracks was becoming ever harder. To make matters worse, John Player withdrew their support at the end of the season. The racing department was subdued at the end of 1974 but there was one bright light on the horizon. The all-new racing engine was due for delivery during 1975.

Desperate Days

The updated engines fitted to the 1973 models helped to restore some confidence in the Commando range. The modifications also enabled Norton to 'stretch' the capacity of the twin-cylinder engine once again. By increasing the bore from 73 to 77mm the capacity was boosted to 829cc. The larger engine was not much more powerful than the 750cc version but it was a little more flexible. It also enabled Norton's engineers to meet new noise and emission requirements with no subsequent loss of performance. All three models were available with the new engine. For marketing reasons it was referred to as an 850. Later in the year, the 750cc engine option was dropped.

To tie in with the racing effort a limited edition John Player Norton 'replica' was produced. It was fitted with a three-quarter-length fairing in the race team's colours and the usual production racer accoutrements. It was available with the 850cc engine or a short-stroke 750cc engine. This used the same bore as the 850 but had an 80.4mm stroke. The short-stroke engine was produced to provide the race team with a more suitable racing engine. The John Player Norton had a short life: it was dropped from the range in 1975.

There were few changes made to the 1974 models but a new logo began to appear on the bikes. By this time Norton Villiers had merged with BSA Triumph and the new company was known variously as Norton Villiers Triumph or Norton Triumph. The stylized initials 'NT' represented the new incarnation. The Commando and the Triumph Trident began to appear in adverts together, the accompanying slogan urging the prospective customer to 'Buy British'. Patriotism is the last refuge of a desperate advertiser and NVT were in trouble. The merger had not gone smoothly, to say the least, and the company's future was uncertain. Despite this, NVT introduced some major changes in 1975. The range was reduced to two models: the Interstate and the Roadster, now in their MkIII guises. Both bikes were fitted with left-foot gear changes to meet American requirements and, to satisfy American requests, electric starters. The starters were not quite up to the job of turning over a large twin-cylinder engine like the Commando's, especially in cold weather. However, they would work if the conditions were favourable (fully charged battery, warm weather, warm bike) and they improved the Commando's specification, at least. Other additions to the specification included a rear disc brake, hydraulic primary chain tensioner and vernier adjustment of the Isolastic mountings. This last feature made adjustment of the Isolastic mountings easier and more accurate. It was to have been included on the first Commandos but it had been replaced by the use of shims, which were fiddlier but much cheaper.

The last of the line? Electric start (sic), left-foot gearchange, annular discharge silencers and detuned engine for the 1975 Mk3 Roadster. In fact, over 130 improvements on the previous model but not enough to save the company from going under. NVT continued to sell 'the last batch' for the next three years.

The Mk III Interstate in late 1973. The 5½ gallon (24.75 litre) petrol tank was a useful item on a touring bike but it was too wide for comfort. This combined with the footrest and handlebar positions made the bike painful to ride. Various alterations were made but the ideal arrangement was never obtained.

The Cosworth Twin

Although the Commando was selling well in the early 1970s, Dennis Poore knew that it could not last forever. A replacement was needed. He asked Tony Denniss to come up with some ideas for a totally new twin-cylinder 750. Denniss worked out some rough ideas and began to see if there were any suitable components which could be bought 'off the shelf' in an attempt to keep development costs down. He found that pistons and valves from a Cosworth racing engine would be ideal. It made sense to use such items since the engine had a good reputation and two cylinders of the three-litre V8 would provide a good basis for a 750cc twin. Poore's reaction was characteristic: 'Let's not waste time. Buy an engine, chop off two cylinders and get to work.' Denniss was not too sure: a Formula 1 Cosworth engine would not be cheap and how would Cosworth feel about Norton 'chopping up' one of their engines? Denniss phoned Cosworth's Chief Designer, Keith Duckworth and told him of the plan. The line went quiet. Eventually, Duckworth said: 'The engines are very expensive . . . £13,000 each.' Denniss relayed the news to Poore. He told Denniss: 'I'll meet you at Cosworth's in forty-five minutes.' After some discussion, Keith Duckworth agreed to design a complete engine for Norton based on the V8. Poore agreed to the price: 'around £40,000' and the matter was sealed over a drink in a nearby pub. (Poore had decided on a twin cylinder engine for a number of reasons but he did hedge his bets: he also commissioned a four cylinder 750cc engine to be built – by BRM of all people. However, Norton ran into serious financial problems and this project was dropped. There were rumours of at least one prototype being produced.)

Rescued by Bob Graves in the eighties, the Cosworth engine realized its potential. In its Quantel form the engine produced 120bhp, power that could have turned the Norton racer into a winner. If only . . .

Production of the Commando was stopped in 1975 when Government aid to the company was refused. A number of bikes were assembled over the next two years but the Commando had come to the end of the line. There was a move to resurrect it the following year but Norton's future lay elsewhere.

Intervention and Interference

Although Norton's future had looked rosy at the beginning of the 1970s, the same could not be said for their rivals BSA Triumph. In 1971 they had reduced the workforce at their Small Heath factory from 4,500 to 1,500 on advice from consultant accountants. If anything this decision made the company less viable and they recorded losses of £4 million for that year. Unable to find finance to rejuvenate the company and with the threatened withdrawal of their overdraft facility, the company's Chairman, Lord Shawcross, turned to the Government for help. They asked the Department of Trade and Industry for financial aid under the recently formed Industry Act, but the accountants who vetted such applications had doubts about BSA Triumph's future, even with Government aid. They suggested a merger with Norton Villiers. It was an idea that Lord Shawcross had considered and one to which he was not opposed. The DTI approached Dennis Poore with the idea in the autumn of 1972. Poore was not too keen on the idea initially but was persuaded that the merger, backed by Government aid, would produce a stronger British motorcycle industry. The proposed merger was agreed in March 1973 and by July that year it was completed. The new company was called Norton Villiers Triumph.

The Government's intervention and its financial assistance were questioned but the minister concerned, Christopher Chataway, argued that it was in the nation's interest to support the British motorcycle industry. Cynics pointed out that it might also be in the Conservative government's interest to provide assistance in an area where the local MP had a slender majority.

The DTI became shareholders in the new company and contributed £5 million. It was a sum that was one-sixth of what Dennis Poore had calculated would be needed to return the industry to an acceptable level of profitability within six years. Still, he had the backing of the Government. Poore's plan for NVT involved closing one of BSA Triumph's two factories and concentrating production at the remaining site. After examining BSA Triumph's accounts it was decided that the Triumph factory at Meriden would have to be closed. There was enough space at the old BSA factory at Small Heath to absorb Triumph's production and even allow the intended expansion. Such a move would save £4 million – equivalent to BSA's annual loss. When the plan was announced to the workforce at Meriden they responded with an immediate blockade of the factory and a demand for continued employment.

The blockade lasted over eighteen months, far longer than anyone could have expected. It occurred during a time of unusually poor labour relations throughout British industry. The situation was further complicated by a miners' strike during the winter of 1973 which resulted in a three-day working week for British industry. This caused lost production for NVT at Small Heath and Wolverhampton and increased the burden on NVT's finances. It also resulted in a general election. Negotiations were halted during the campaign period because the politicians involved were too busy with other matters. The Conservatives lost to the Labour Party in February 1974, and Tony Benn became the minister in charge of the new Trade Department. His radical ideals led him to support the blockaders and he actively encouraged them in their plans to establish a co-operative at Meriden. Despite advice by civil servants working for the Department of Trade, and other members of the Government, he also offered financial assistance to establish the co-operative.

Negotiations continued, interrupted by another general election in October 1974, which provided the Labour Party with a majority (something they had not had previously). More negotiations finally produced a plan that was acceptable to Dennis Poore, Tony Benn and the men at Meriden. However, the Small Heath workers did not agree with it. Small Heath had experienced heavy redundancies in 1971 and Meriden had offered them little sympathy at the time, despite Meriden's militant reputation and their readiness to help other worthy causes. Initial attempts by Benn to talk the BSA workers round met with little success. At one meeting at Small Heath he was chased out of the factory. His support for Meriden at the expense of the BSA workers was not appreciated! Other unions were persuaded to put pressure on the BSA workforce and they eventually agreed to the latest plan. This resulted in a co-operative being established at Meriden with Government loans and a small grant. A large part of the capital was used to buy the premises, plant and any unfinished bikes at Meriden. Meriden would produce the Bonneville and NVT would sell it alongside the Trident, which was produced at Small Heath. The co-operative came into being in March 1975.

The worst was not over for NVT, however. The booming motorcycle market that had existed up to 1974 collapsed in 1975. The Japanese were heavily overstocked, particularly in America. A price war erupted and NVT could not compete. Furthermore, the Export Credit Guarantee Department, which provided a kind of bridging loan for exporters, refused to help them. NVT applied to the Department of Trade for assistance under the Industry Act. By this time, June 1975, Tony Benn had been replaced by Eric Varley. NVT might have expected assistance from Benn, for, even though he had taken Meriden's side in the dispute, NVT were responsible for marketing the co-operative's products. Eric Varley, however, was a different matter. More realistic than idealistic, Varley believed that further aid would only delay the inevitable. The application was refused.

The refusal signalled the end of the road for Norton Villiers Triumph. The 'inevitable' came quickly. Production at Small Heath and Wolverhampton was halted and redundancy notices were issued. A small workforce was retained to complete assembly of any unfinished bikes and assist the liquidators. The company was wound down over the next few years but the Norton name did not disappear altogether. Various service companies were set up to organize the sale and distribution of the remaining stock and to provide spare parts for Norton and Triumph machines. Dennis Poore established a small off-shoot at Shenstone in Staffordshire to continue development of a number of projects which had been in progress at the company's research establishment (at Kitt's Green). Norton Villiers Triumph was no more but it was not quite the end of the Norton story.

6

Rotary Revival

A Mixed Assortment

There had been a number of projects in the pipeline at Norton and BSA Triumph in the early 1970s. With the collapse of NVT, Dennis Poore had obtained the rights to some of them. He set about establishing a small research and manufacturing facility in an empty meat-packing factory owned by Manganese Bronze Holdings in Staffordshire. One of the projects was an air-cooled Wankel engine which BSA had been developing for motorcycle use. Although this was a long-term proposition there were others which could quickly be put into production.

The Norton Triumph International research establishment at Kitt's Green had produced a design for a moped using many bought-in components. Moped sales were still buoyant in 1976, so it was decided to go into production. It was, perhaps, a two-wheeled 'pot-boiler', but it was no worse than many mopeds then available. It was assembled at Shenstone but both the frame and the Franco Morini two-stroke engine were made in Italy. Sold as the NVT Easy Rider, it was available in five different forms with a choice of single-speed, two-speed or four-speed gearbox. It was joined in 1977 by another Kitt's Green design, a 125cc trail bike called the Rambler. This had cantilever or 'monoshock' rear suspension which was just becoming fashionable and a front disc brake (which was unique amongst trail bikes). The

cycle parts came from Italy but the engine was Japanese: a single-cylinder two-stroke unit, made by Yamaha, and one of the best around. Bob Trigg, one of the development team, later went to work for Yamaha at their European headquarters in Holland. Through him the link with the Japanese firm was strengthened. It was a link which would prove advantageous to Norton in many ways over the coming years.

Nearly, but not quite. Using a Suzuki TS125 engine, this prototype was considered for production but instead NVT chose another partner for their 'marriage of Eastern and Western technology'. The Rambler used a Yamaha 125cc engine and was the first trail bike to have a disc brake.

The assembly of these models (and a child's 'fun bike' called the Junior) was easily accommodated within the spacious Shenstone factory. Their sales generated an income of sorts and allowed a production facility to be created. Other projects followed. One of these involved modifying Yamaha XS750s to make them suitable for police use; another was the production of the Yamaha HL500. This was a single-cylinder 500cc four-stroke motocrosser, a copy of the bike that had given works' Yamaha rider Bengt Aberg his sole

A practical sort of boffin, David Garside graduated from Emmanuel College, Cambridge with a first-class honours degree in Mechanical Sciences Tripos and won the prize for the best paper in Thermodynamics. He worked on diesel rotary design at Rolls Royce Motor Cars before joining BSA in 1969. He is Britain's leading authority on rotary technology and responsible for the development of the family of engines produced by Norton and used in marine, aviation and motorcycling applications.

moto cross Grand Prix success. Norton built 400 of them for Yamaha in 1978 and 1979. Norton's contact at Yamaha for this project was Richard Negus. Negus had worked for Norton Triumph International at Kitt's Green before being made redundant; he was to return to Norton Motors in 1982 and take a leading role in motorcycle production.

Rotary Research and Development

Production of the mopeds and the 125s continued at Shenstone until 1978, when it was moved to another factory which MBH owned at Garretts Green. (Production of the smaller machine was later taken over by Bill Colquhoun and they were sold under the BSA name.) Dennis Poore had become dissatisfied with the progress of the Wankel-engined bike and, on being told that the production bikes were taking up too much of the development team's time, had the distraction removed. In fact, there was more to it than that. Like all development engineers, David Garside was unwilling to present a definitive production version when there was still scope for improvement. There was also the question of prototype testing; no one wanted to put into production a bike that had not been thoroughly tested, and thorough testing was an expensive and time-consuming business. Tony Denniss came up with a solution: a prototype was loaned to the West Midlands Police Force for assessment. Their riders regularly clocked up high mileages and they would be able to make objective reports on the bike's behaviour.

The reports must have been favourable. After six months' testing, the force asked to be supplied with the new bike for regular police use. Dennis Poore was not keen on the idea; perhaps it went against the image he had in mind for the bike. He was persuaded otherwise and in 1981 a batch of twenty-five bikes was made. These were fitted with BMW-style fairings and other items to make them suitable for police work. Following on from the police-issue Commando, the Interpol, the new bike was called the Interpol II. It was the first model to be produced by the new Norton company. (When NVT had collapsed the Norton name had been one of the assets retained by the receivers. Dennis Poore bought the name back and, at Tony Denniss's suggestion, the new company was named Norton Motors (1978) Ltd, a name recalling an earlier incarnation.)

It was not long before other police forces wanted the Interpol II. Although it had not been the intention to produce a bike for police duty there were advantages to doing so. Firm orders and batch production would suit small-scale manufacturing and enable the company to build up a 'pilot' production line. Fleet use would mean that instead of widespread individual ownership and related servicing problems there would be clusters of bikes with ready access to properly trained mechanics: a perfect situation for a new design. The idea was appealing, and Norton made the bike available to the British police and the armed services. Two presentation days were organized, at Donington and Thruxton race circuits. Interested parties were invited along and, to add a little spice, the factory displayed another model. This was one of the new bikes in a very different guise, intended as a record-breaker. An attempt on some long-distance records was planned to show the bike's potential and its durability, but in the end nothing ever came of it. Norton did get plenty of orders for the Interpol II, though, and the record-breaker sowed the seeds for a future project.

Police experience with the Interpol II proved valuable to the development team. The bikes were often used alongside BMWs, which provided a useful yardstick: the rotary had always been seen in the same league as the BMW, if not above it. The rotary was much more responsive than the BMW, it was smoother and had better top-end performance, but it was very rough at the bottom end of the rev range. This was one of the characteristics of the Wankel engine and was emphasized by the peculiar demands of urban police work, where extended periods of low-speed running were often encountered. There were other minor problems too, indicating that more work had to be done before the bike would be ready for general release. To help solve some of these problems Norton called on a man who had worked for them twice

The Interpol II was supplied to the police, the Army and the RAC. In fact, the RAC were the largest single buyer. Unfortunately, police and RAC use was not representative of normal motorcycling conditions. Such use did, however, emphasize the need to improve the rotary's low-speed characteristics.

The Rotary Engine

Norton's rotary engine began life as a BSA project at their research establishment at Umberslade Hall in 1969. Dennis Poore saw the engine's potential following the NVT merger and ensured its continued development. Its eventual success was due to the distinguished engineer who lead the development team – David Garside.

The engine that powers the Interpol II and the Classic is an air-cooled, twin rotor unit but it also forms the basis for the water-cooled engines. Wankel engines have little in common with piston engines and the Norton engine is no exception. The eccentric mainshaft is a hardened steel forging supported by two roller bearings and located axially by a smaller ball-race on the right side. Being of a large diameter, the eccentric is exceptionally strong and resistant to flexing. It carries a pair of 'triangular' cast-iron rotors. Each rotor has a 'radius' of 71mm (2.8in) and is 68.2mm (2.7in) wide; the mainshaft has an eccentricity of 11.6mm (0.46in). The peanut-shaped trochoidal chambers are alloy castings and their wearing faces are coated with a special 'Elnisil' coating to give them a long life. The side-plates are made of a high silicon-content aluminium alloy. The rotor seals – generally regarded as a weak point in rotary engines – were perfected by Norton with assistance from Mazda. They are made of IKA 3 cast iron and are very hard wearing. The rotor's path around the chamber is controlled by inverted gear teeth inside the rotor mating with a fixed gear attached to one of the side-plates. A roller bearing supports the rotor on the shaft. The internal surfaces of the rotor are cooled by air which is drawn through ports in the side-plates as part of the induction system. The resultant warm air is cooled in a plenum chamber before it reaches the carburettors (the racing engine uses a slightly different system). Other rotary engines have oil-cooled rotors, but by perfecting air-cooling, Norton have produced an engine which loses very little energy through friction – much less even than a reciprocating engine of comparable power.

The eccentric movement of the rotor within the trochoid housing creates three chambers of continually changing volumes. The petrol/air mixture is drawn in through ports in the face of the housing at the 'two o'clock' position. The rotor moves round the chamber anticlockwise, compressing the mixture until it is ignited by the spark plugs in the 'nine o'clock' position. The expanding gas forces the rotor to continue moving and is exhausted through a port in the 'four o'clock' position.

A high-power generator on the left end of the eccentric shaft provides electrical power. Ignition is provided by a Norton Hall-effect system which fires the single surface discharge spark plug in each chamber. A small sprocket on the right end of the eccentric drives the primary chain. The clutch is a diaphragm unit and the gearbox is a mixture of Triumph and Norton design. (On the F1 this is replaced by a Yamaha gear cluster.) A variable-stroke oil-metering pump is driven by the gearbox shaft and oil is fed into the induction air stream. This is enough to lubricate the bearings and all rubbing surfaces. It is a total-loss system (as in modern two-stroke engines).

The power output of the Classic and the Interpol II was around 75bhp, the F1 produced nearer 90bhp and the racer produced 140bhp at the end of 1989. They all used basically the same engine. All three engines use the same components; as with two-stroke engines the induction and exhaust systems and the shape, size and distribution of the inlet and exhaust ports are important. In comparison with a reciprocating engine of similar power output, the Norton rotary is smaller, simpler and smoother. The majority of problems that have bedevilled the rotary combustion engine in general have been overcome (and not just by Norton). Prejudice and ignorance have held back the rotary engine's acceptance and continue to do so, as does the massive capital outlay that would be required before a major manufacturer could go into production with such an engine. For Norton, starting from scratch in the late 1970s, it was not such a great problem.

Twin chamber rotary engine as fitted to the Norton Interpol 2 Police Motorcycle

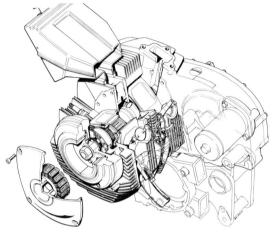

The Wankel rotary combustion engine is so unlike the reciprocating piston engine that comparisons complicate more than they clarify. The rotary engine ran for the first time in 1957 and in comparison with the reciprocating engine, the design is still in its youthful stage.

Chamber capacity	588cc	
Power output (kW)	63 (85bhp) at 9,000rpm	
Compression ratio	9.0:1	
Fuel	97octane 4star (leaded) petrol	
Clutch	9 plate sintered bronze 9 intermediate plain plates Diaphragm spring operated	
Gearbox	5-speed constant mesh	
Carburettors	Twin SU H1F4 constant vacuum 1½in dia choke-temperature compensated	

		From Engine No. 3110
Engine sprocket teeth	30	
Clutch sprocket teeth	57	
Gearbox sprocket teeth	18	17
Rear wheel sprocket teeth	42	43
Overall ratio	4.43	4.81
Engine rpm at 10mph in top gear	606	658

Doug Hele was first interviewed for a job with Norton by Joe Craig in 1947 at Bracebridge Street. He worked with Bert Hopwood and later joined him at BSA; both men returned in the mid-fifties before moving to Triumph (where Hele played an important role in improving Triumph's range and developing the Trident). Hele returned to Norton in 1982 to assist in 'productionizing' the Interpol II.

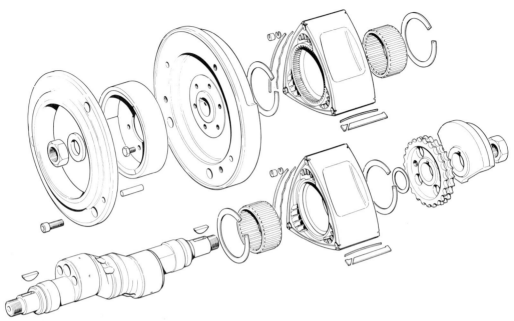

The twin triangular rotors of the Wankel rotary are needle-roller mounted at 180 degrees to each other on the forged eccentric shaft housed within the aluminium trochoid chambers. This provides the progressive phases of the four-cycle combustion sequence on each of the three rotor flanks. The eccentric shaft incorporates horizontally bored cooling air ducts with the rotors featuring internally cast cooling fins which ensure internal thermal stability.

before, Doug Hele. He had also worked for BSA Triumph on some of the very early versions of the rotary engine. He returned in 1982 to advise on design and development. In all, around 400 Interpol IIs were produced between 1981 and 1987. In some ways the company considered the Interpol II a distraction. It did not represent the form the intended production motorcycle would take and it absorbed too much of the small factory's time and facilities. However, it did provide Norton with a 'pilot' situation enabling them to examine any potential problems before going into full-scale production.

Norton continued to develop the rotary combustion engine throughout the early 1980s. The West Midlands force tested a water-cooled version, the Interpol IIA, and

another water-cooled prototype was seen in the motorcycle magazines when Norton lent it to their German distributors. Water-cooling was being considered in an attempt to find a solution to the problem of overheating encountered during low-speed police work. It had other advantages too. Removal of the extensive finning brought about a considerable weight saving and the water-cooling jacket reduced the engine noise – an environmental consideration which would be important in later years. For the time being, though, production bikes continued to be air-cooled. Norton also began to look at other applications for the rotary combustion engine in the early 1980s. Possibilities considered included light aircraft use, outboard motors and lightweight generators.

Revival

Manganese Bronze had been financing the company since the move to Shenstone in 1975 and during that time it had not returned a profit. By the mid-1980s, around £4 million had been absorbed. Throughout this period Dennis Poore had been taking an active interest in the company as well as directing Manganese Bronze in his capacity as Chairman. His involvement with his other business interests and increasing worries about ill-health (he was 69 in 1985) led him to bring in Dennis Austin to run Norton. Austin had been a director of Lotus Cars and had been instrumental in helping Poore buy back the block of shares still owned by the Government (a legacy of their 'assistance' in forming NVT).

Free from the interference of politicians and civil servants and with a motorcycle ready to go into production, Poore and Austin considered the future. Poore believed that the company was not in a position to go back into business on its own. He wanted to find a company with compatible interests, facilities or experience and merge the two to provide support for Norton during its critical re-emergence. Unfortunately there was no suitable company to be found in Britain in the 1980s. Towards the end of 1985, with no one to take Norton on as a working company and with his health deteriorating, Dennis Poore was forced to begin putting the company into liquidation.

The existing shareholders of Norton Villiers Triumph Ltd were given the opportunity of cashing in their virtually worthless shares or exchanging them for shares in a new company called The Norton Villiers Triumph Group PLC. NVTG was a shell company involved in property dealing, but it too ran into trouble. A new Managing Director with a sound background in finance was appointed:

Philippe Le Roux. Initially he was unaware of the existence of the motorcycle division and was surprised to learn that it not only existed but was still making motorcycles – albeit in the hands of the receiver. This knowledge coupled with a growing awareness of the value of the Norton name led him to investigate further. Le Roux contacted Poore to learn more about the work that had been carried out at Shenstone and discuss the possible uses for Norton's Wankel engine technology. By February 1987 Le Roux was convinced that

Philippe Le Roux: 'the man who liked the name so much, he bought the company.' Actually, the rotary technology also appealed. An unlikely saviour but one who appreciated the need to go beyond motorcycle production in order to safeguard the company's future.

there was a future for Norton. He exchanged the NVTG property interests for the motorcycle business and its related rotary technology. He invested his own money, raised more capital from the present shareholders and raised a further £2 million from a public subscription. In all, £3.7 million was raised within a few months.

A Classic Norton

One of the first things Philippe Le Roux did on taking control of the company was to get a motorcycle pushed into production for the public. The bike was being tested by the motorcycle press during the summer of 1987 and the first examples were delivered before the end of the year. The inertia that had delayed such a venture in the past was swept away by the new broom. The bike that was announced, the Classic, was little different from one of the prototypes that had been built back in 1975. It was attacked by some of the motorcycling press for not having ultra-modern styling, for looking like 'a ten year-old Ducati'; less knowledgeable commentators dismissed Norton, saying that they were beating the worn drum of nostalgia. But that was not the case, and the point of the Classic had been missed.

By producing the Classic in such a short time Philippe Le Roux showed that he had galvanized the company into action. Production of the Classic was limited to 100 machines, guaranteeing that they would be snapped up by collectors if no one else. Its styling in this case was immaterial, but to prove that Norton's designers did not have their heads in the sand details of an up-to-date touring bike were also released. Production of the Classic fulfilled two functions: it brought Norton an immediate income (100 motorcycles at

£5,950 each is easy arithmetic) and it cleared away stocks of air-cooled engines. Future Nortons were to be water-cooled.

The Classic surprised a lot of people by being an excellent motorcycle. Not surprising really, considering the years of development that had gone into it. Its looks were old-fashioned but it was still attractive. Its handling was impressive and the only real fault was that the centre stand or the large (police-issue) footrests would touch the ground too easily. It was quite a heavy bike at 500lb (227kg) but its weight was not apparent. The low centre of gravity provided by the rotary engine's layout contributed to the bike's handling and made it manageable at low speeds. Norton claimed that the engine produced 80bhp at 7,000rpm, which was probably optimistic, but it was incredibly flexible throughout the rev range. The rotary engine was much more responsive than any piston engine in the higher gears, and power output increased smoothly in any gear in direct proportion to throttle opening. Such behaviour made the Classic an ideal bike to ride through twisty roads once the rider had become accustomed to it. The lack of engine braking, which is a characteristic of rotary engines, was disconcerting at first but the brakes were able to compensate for it. Top speed was around 125mph (200kph). A rev-limiter was incorporated in the electronic ignition, operating at 9,000rpm. It was a necessary item: acceleration was rapid and the engine so smooth that it would be very easy to over-rev the engine. A limiting factor for the engine revs was the transmission. Development engines had shown an ability to rev to 14,000rpm in safety but the primary drive-chain and the gearbox were not capable of standing up to such speeds. It was not a problem for the road bike but would become one should Norton go racing.

The Classic

The Classic was the first rotary-engined Norton to be made available to the public. It used the air-cooled engine which had been evaluated over the previous six years by various police forces and the Ministry of Defence. It had a box-section spine frame made up from 1.5mm thick steel pressings. This was designed by Bob Trigg in the early 1970s for a prototype which was very similar in appearance to the Classic. Although it was considered old-fashioned in 1987, it was still effective and continued to be used for the Commander (where fully-enclosed bodywork prevented the frame from upsetting delicate sensibilities).

The rotary engine was a revelation – much smoother than any piston engine and with an incredibly wide spread of power. Top speed was around 130mph (208kph) with a standing quarter-mile time of just under 12 seconds. The Classic's performance was similar to that of an average middleweight Japanese bike or a large four-cylinder BMW. Possibly the only drawback was poor fuel consumption. When used enthusiastically, the Classic would return under 40mpg (1,415km/100l).

The Classic gave some indication of the rotary engine's potential. However, despite the low weight of the rotary engine it was not an unusually lightweight bike: at 500lb (230kg) it weighed about the same as a 1,000cc BMW and much more than a 600cc Honda four. A low centre of gravity – possible due to the rotary engine's format – helped to disguise this shortcoming. Still, the Classic was an excellent motorcycle – if it had been produced in the mid-1970s, when it was first designed, it would have been sensational. It was produced as a limited edition model and only 100 were produced, in 1987 and 1988. The two models that followed – the Commander and the F1 – gave a better indication of Norton's direction.

The Classic. The first rotary-engined Norton to go on sale to the public was criticized unnecessarily for its 'dated' styling.

The Commander

Production of the water-cooled model, called the Commander, began before the last of the Classics was delivered. Its styling was modern without being outrageous, and aimed directly at the BMW-type tourer market. Philippe Le Roux wanted Norton motorcycles to be a two-wheeled equivalent of Jaguar cars (an ideal he shared with Dennis Poore). The Commander fitted the bill. The job of producing the first Commanders was given to Richard Negus. Like Doug Hele, he too had been involved with the rotary engine in its early days at BSA. He had also worked for Norton at Andover and Kitt's Green before going to work for Yamaha in Europe. He

Richard Negus had worked on the earliest prototypes of the rotary engine (including the first Fichtel and Sachs engined B25). He eventually became responsible for general motorcycle production at Norton. In the seventies he even raced a Commando in the World Endurance Championships.

returned in 1982 to run the spares division but was asked to take on construction of the Commander in 1987. He was later put in overall charge of motorcycle production.

A comprehensive fairing and fibreglass bodywork enclosed the new model and built-in panniers added to the touring specification. The bike was painted a restrained 'Dorchester grey', with the Norton logo in red on the petrol tank and fairing. The fairing concealed the engine, much smaller now it was devoid of its 4-inch fins, but otherwise much the same internally as the earlier version. The frame was the same sheet-metal fabrication that had been used on the Classic and the Interpol II but altered slightly to accommodate new cycle parts. The earlier models had used Italian front forks, brakes and wheels but the new bike used Japanese items, Yamaha XJ900 parts. The same firm also supplied the instruments, the switch-gear and other electrical components. The use of Japanese components irritated some British 'enthusiasts' but their use was an economic necessity. There were no suitable British suppliers, the quality of the Japanese items was superior and there were no problems with delivery dates, changes in specification or price fluctuations. The first civilian Commander was presented to the motorcyling press at the Isle of Man TT in 1988. The bike was finished in the early hours of the morning and run in on the way to the Island. It was well received by the press and considered to be eligible for the 'super-tourer' bracket. Its Jaguar-class status was reflected in its price: £7,945.

Rotary Racing

As well as the Classic and the Commander, Philippe Le Roux had sanctioned another project which began to make the news in

Produced as a police patrol bike or a civilian tourer, the Commander gave a better indication of Norton's direction. Front forks, wheels and electrics came from Yamaha's XJ900.

1987. In their own time, two of Norton's staff, Brian Crighton and Dave Evans, had been trying their hands at tuning the rotary engine. Crighton had a successful racing background and the rotary engine interested him. The engine responded to basic two-stroke tuning methods and he was quickly convinced of its potential. However, racing was low down on Norton's list of priorities until Crighton showed the bike's potential to Le Roux in July 1987. A crudely converted police bike was taken up to 170mph (270kph) at the MIRA testing grounds and the Norton racer was born. Within six weeks the first purpose-built Norton rotary racer was seen on the tracks. Two weeks after that it won its first race, ridden by Norton employee Malcolm Heath. Admittedly it was only a club meeting but it helped to reinforce the message that Norton had overcome the inertia that had gripped the company for so long.

The new racer was very different from the road-going bikes. The frame was an aluminium 'beam frame' built by Spondon Engineering. The two main frame spars ran down from the steering-head to the rear of the engine, where they dog-legged behind the gearbox. The triangulated rear fork was attached at this point and controlled by an Olins gas-filled shock absorber. The engine was suspended beneath the main frame and attached at two points at the rear (which incorporated the swinging-arm spindle) and two points at the front. Front suspension was handled by Japanese Kayaba forks and the brakes were a mixture of Brembo and Spondon components. All the cycle parts – including the Honda RS250 petrol tank and seat and the Dymag alloy wheels – were 'standard race-wear' to provide the team with fewer unknown quantities in the new bike. Unfortunately the unique characteristics of the rotary engine were to affect the suspension and handling of the bike in a manner which no one expected.

The engines used in the racer were often built up from components rejected during the stringent quality control assessments which had recently been introduced at the factory (part of the Civil Aviation Authority's certification requirements for Norton's light-aircraft engine). Power output was around 135bhp at 9,500rpm from an engine which appeared little different from the road bike's unit. Brian Crighton modestly claimed that the power increase was achieved through application of basic two-stroke tuning principles. The only major alteration to the road bike engine was in the induction system. On the road bikes the induction air was used to cool the engine internals before it reached the carburettors. This meant that the engine was being fed with warm air, which restricted its efficiency. On the racer, the carburettors were fed directly from inlets at the front of the fairing. The hollow rotors were still cooled internally, but the air flow was achieved by what Crighton called an 'ejector exhaust' system. The exhaust system incorporated a venturi section which created a low-pressure area as the exhaust gas travelled through it. A pipe from this point was connected to the side-plate of the rotary engine and formed part of an airway through the rotors. A pair of small air-scoops on the fairing were connected to the other end of this path and, when the bike was moving, created a high-pressure 'feed'. The resultant imbalance provided an efficient flow of cool air through the engine. Oil used to lubricate the internals of the engine escaped with the air but the very high temperature of the exhaust gas caused immediate ignition. The resultant 'flame-thrower' effect was highly entertaining.

The RC588, as the racer was called, weighed about 300lb (136kg), approximately 45lb (20kg) less than a 500cc Grand Prix bike. The engine weighed about 120lb and produced 130bhp, enough to make the bike competitive in the Formula One and 750cc classes in which it was raced. There were few significant differences from the standard engine. Amal smoothbore carburettors replaced the SUs used on the road bikes and a Norton-developed 'Hall effect' ignition system replaced the standard CDI. In some ways the rotary engine behaves like a two-stroke, and its power output can be controlled accordingly. The racing engine's chief increase in power was obtained by altered port-timing,

just as in a two-stroke. The ejector exhaust system was responsible for improved engine cooling, although it also improved the efficiency of the induction system.

The unconventional nature of the rotary engine has caused problems in the past and continues to do so. Its progress has been bedevilled by wild claims made by its detractors. Political and economic considerations have had as much part in its development as engineering applications. The determination of the capacity of a rotary engine has always been a problem due, chiefly, to each 'cylinder' having three separate chambers (rotary engines with more than three chambers are also possible). Argument, both informed and uninformed, led to a 1.4:1 handicap being applied to rotary engines used in car racing (the actual capacity of the engine being multiplied by 1.4 to give a 'permitted' capacity to determine in which class it may compete). Norton were given a 'dispensation' by the ACU to run their bike in certain classes at national level in Britain, and the FIM followed suit, allowing it to race in international Formula One events. These events were open to roadster-derived 750cc four-stroke fours and 1000cc four-stroke twins. Unlike its car racing counterpart, motorcycle Formula One racing in the late 1980s was 'third division' racing. However, this arrangement suited Norton, as they were still learning about the rotary engine. They also lacked the experience of running a race team and, more importantly, they had only limited sponsorship in 1988. It was something of a probationary period, during which Norton, their rivals and the FIM would learn much about the rotary's racing potential.

There were no fairy-tale successes in 1988 for the Norton race team. It was a case of hard work and perserverance. Works' riders Trevor Nation and Simon Buckmaster had a disappointing time in the Senior TT at the Isle of Man that year. The bikes' handling gave them a hard time and there were more than enough minor problems to keep them occupied. Despite this, both bikes finished and Nation managed to lap at over 115mph (184kph). The handling problems which afflicted the bike were found to be caused by the rotary engine's peculiar power delivery. On the exit from a corner, the rear suspension would 'squat', compressed by the abundance of torque from the engine. On bumpy tracks and the Isle of Man this was particularly undesirable. It took some time to find a remedy, but by raising the engine, shortening the wheelbase and fitting specially built White Power front forks and rear suspension the problem was overcome. On its first outing the revised RC588 was ridden to a new Formula One lap record by Trevor Nation. Its first victory followed a week later at Carnaby in Yorkshire when the bike was ridden by Andy

A more professional image came with sponsorship from John Player early in 1988. The agreement, rumoured to be worth £750,000 enabled Norton to aim for a return to Grand Prix racing.

The F1

The F1 was produced in 1990 as a replica of Norton's rotary racer. In fact, it had first appeared as a prototype almost two years earlier. With the success of the factory race team, the bike was restyled and produced in the colours of the team's sponsors, John Player cigarettes.

The F1 used an aluminium twin-spar beam frame built by Spondon Engineering and very similar to the racer's frame. 'Upside-down' White Power forks and a White Power rear suspension unit were also common features to the two bikes. PVM cast alloy wheels and Brembo discs contributed to the high-quality specification of the bike.

The F1's engine was an advanced version of the type used in the racer up to 1990 (homologation rules prevented Norton from using the later type engine until 200 units had been produced). The chief difference was the use of a Yamaha FZR1000 gearbox, which was much stronger than the original Norton Triumph hybrid. Unfortunately, the ratios in the new gearbox were not fully suited to the F1's engine characteristics which spoilt the bike's performance. Also, the FZR1000 used gear primary drive but the F1 used twin primary chains. This meant that the direction of rotation of the Norton engine had to be reversed – a relatively easy operation for a rotary engine and one which improved both the inlet and exhaust systems.

The F1 used two 34mm down-draft Mikuni carburettors and altered port timing which enabled the engine to produce a claimed 95bhp at 9,500rpm. In fact, one popular motorcycle magazine measured the F1's power output, at the back wheel, at 77.5bhp, but this was similar to the power produced by the best Japanese sports 600s (manufacturer's figures are notoriously unreliable). However the F1 had a wider spread of power than many 750s, making it an easier bike to ride and just as fast across country as 'more powerful' bikes. The same magazine gave the F1's top speed as 144.5mph (231kph). The handling was considered good and excellent even, once the suspension was adjusted to suit personal requirements. The overall finish was also praised, but the F1 was hand-built and expensive. It cost £12,700.

McGladdery. There were other wins and lap records throughout the year, but only one at international level. However, the season ended on a positive note: Steve Spray, riding the RC588 for the first time, won the Powerbike International at Brands Hatch. His performance was seen by potential sponsors, Imperial Tobacco, and it was good enough to convince them. In January 1988 a three-year deal, believed to be worth £750,000, was announced. The team would race in the John Player Special colours of black, grey and gold.

The sponsorship agreement allowed the race team to move out of their cramped surroundings – the converted kitchen of a semi-detached house in the factory grounds – and into a spacious purpose-built workshop. Production of over 200 Commanders had been achieved in 1988, meeting homologation requirements for the water-cooled engine. A water-cooled version of the racer, the RCW588, was unveiled for the new season. In an effort to reduce front wheel lift, the direction of rotation of the new engine was reversed. This, and the myriad modifications which are part of race development, boosted the bike's performance, enabling Steve Spray to win the British Formula One Championship and the Shell Oils Supercup. Trevor Nation had a run of bad luck that year but still managed to pick up a handful of firsts and lap records.

The F1

A super-sports version of the rotary racer had been seen at the Earls Court Motorcycle Show in October 1988. This version used the same frame and cycle parts as the racer but did not have the ejector exhaust system or the improved carburation. The bodywork enclosed the bike completely but lacked the aggressive angularity of most race-replicas. The Dorchester grey paintwork of the body was similarly subtle but the bright red alloy wheels saved the bike from looking too subdued. Called the P55, it was something of a show-stopper but was not immediately available. In fact, it was not released until the middle of 1990. Its appearance was altered slightly, it was now called the F1 and it was painted in the racer's colour scheme. Although this spoilt the bike's appearance, it was still a handsome machine.

The F1 cost £12,700. It was one of the most expensive motorcycles available but no one who rode the bike queried the price. It was a handbuilt motorcycle using some of the finest components available. The water-cooled engine produced 90bhp which was enough to give it performance equal to that of the latest Japanese four-cylinder 600s (a fiercely competitive class) and justification of Norton's claim that the engine really was 588cc. The spread of torque from the rotary engine was unlike that encountered on any piston-engined bike and made the F1 easier to ride. A new gearbox was used on the F1, based on a five-speed cluster from the Yamaha FZ1000 (a six-speed option was also available). Although chain primary drive was retained, the possibility of gear drive was accommodated in the design. The F1's styling, handling and performance were considered a match for anything the Italians or the Japanese could produce. Norton Motors' Managing Director, Graham White, said 'We have designed the F1 to be the best super-sports machine in the world.' There were those in the know who said that Norton had succeeded.

Useful Addresses

Anyone who owns or is contemplating owning a Norton is strongly advised to join the Norton Owners' Club – a source of advice, information and hardware. They have a worldwide membership and can be contacted through:

> Ms Shirley Fenner
> 18 Wren Close
> Addlestone
> Surrey
> KT15 2JR

Membership of the Vintage Motor Cycle Club is also recommended:

> V.M.C.C. Ltd.
> 138 Derby Street
> Burton-on-Trent
> Staffordshire
> DE14 2LF

There are a number of sources of spare parts for Nortons in Great Britain and elsewhere. Below is a short list of knowledgeable and helpful suppliers. It is worth knowing that Norton Motors can, of course, supply parts for the rotary-engined models as well as for the Commando variants:

> Norton Motors Ltd
> Lynn Lane
> Shenstone
> Lichfield
> Staffordshire
> WS14 0EA

Fair Spares is a very helpful company and, in addition to being able to supply standard components, they can also supply genuine Norvil competition parts (and complete replica Norvil racers):

> Fair Spares
> The Corner Garage
> 96–98 Cannock Road
> Chase Terrace
> Burntwood
> Staffordshire
> WS7 8JP
> (Tel: 0543 278008)

Fair Spares have distributors in the USA and Australia:

> Fair Spares America Inc.
> P.O. Box 8224
> San Jose
> California
> 95155
> USA

> Fair Spares Australia
> P.O. Box 185
> Campbelltown
> New South Wales
> 2560
> Australia

Also in Australia is:

Don's Bike Supplies
P.O. Box 1163
Perth
6001

Mick Hemmings specializes in competition
parts for Norton twins but also provides other
services:

Mick Hemmings
36/42 Wellington Street
Northampton
NN1 3AS

Unity Equipe are specialists in Manx Nortons
and associated cycle parts:

Unity Equipe
916 Manchester Road
Castleton
Rochdale
Lancashire

One of the few companies with a decent stock
of parts for the single cylinder models (as well
as the twins) is:

Russell Motors
125–127 Faclon Road
Battersea
London
SW11 2PE

Index